THE NEIGHBORHOOD

THE NEIGHBORHOOD

STORIES. BY KELLY MAGEE.

Gold Wake

TABLE OF CONTENTS

The Merm Prob
3

The Pedestal
13

You Don't Live Here
19

The Stepmothers
38

Dear Fairy Godmother
44

You're Not Going to Die
55

Origin Story
69

The Moral
79

Grandma's House
91

Nobody Understands You Like Us
110

The Neighborhood
123

For my mother, Joy,
who is one of the good ones

THE MERM PROB

When the seas warmed, the mermaids washed ashore. The first one made the news, like you'd expect, and there was a lot of talk about how she didn't look like the storybooks – the fangs, for starters, or the way she spit – but fast forward a few months and we'd all gotten used to the idea. Fast forward a few more months and we wished we'd never seen a mermaid. The live ones were mean, the sick ones were depressing, and the dead ones fouled up the water. We left the clean-up to our husbands. After a while, there was no more talk of burials or vigils or rescue. These weren't beached whales or disoriented sea turtles. They bit. And talk about a racket – when they weren't yelling at each other in their weird, high-pitched language, they were wailing fit to drive us crazy.

We took them into our homes and saltwater pools like foreign exchange students, but they didn't appreciate the favor. They thrashed around and damaged our pool vacs, which already couldn't cope with the amount of waste the mermaids produced. They expelled strings of fish crap like you wouldn't believe. They flopped onto our decks and shredded our privacy fences and wrecked our lawns. Forget flowerbeds. Forget sending your kids to play out back when you needed to breathe or think or bathe. The merms, as we started calling them, didn't understand that they couldn't go back to the sea, that we'd saved them from extinction, and they sure as hell didn't take kindly to domestication.

We were stuck. As good and decent people, we couldn't just exterminate them. We called a series of town meetings to deal with the Merm Prob. We debated. Brainstormed. Our husbands talked about the health hazard the merms posed, and some of us said we ought to throw them back and let them deal. These were the original Good Samaritans, the early adopters whose backyards had become merm cesspools, whose decks were slick with merm shit. You could see the trauma on their faces. *She attacked my dog,* one might say. *Ate the insides and left it on the back porch in a pool of blood. I had that dog before I had kids.* And another, with red-rimmed eyes: *Screw the dog. Watch out for your kids.*

There was trauma. We'd been a peaceful community who never argued over politics or religion, didn't lock our car doors, donated to anti-erosion and pro-pedestrian funds; a racially harmonious town with low interest rates and free popcorn at the megaplex on Tuesdays. We weren't prepared for this. This wasn't the goddamn ocean, we'd say in our low moments. This was *civilization*. This was our *town*. We used to have koi ponds in our backyards with koi named Baby and Sweetheart; we used to have chickens that lived happy chicken lives until they died of natural causes; we used to have neon Drive Carefully! signs with flags to alert drivers who might be having an off day. We all had off days. We didn't judge.

If the merms had ever thrown us a bone – one smile, say, or even just *not* bared their teeth when we fed them – we might be in a whole different situation. But we're not robots. We're not made of steel. We got fed up, and though we might be ashamed to say this now, we began to hate those mermaids.

It pains us to say that some of us invented epithets for them, which we will not repeat here.

Most of us remained civil. It's easy to remember the chaos, the infighting, but the majority of us had our hearts in the right places. That's what we say when we're asked to comment publically. *Our hearts,* we say, tapping our chests. *In the right places.*

At the town meetings, we emphasized the merms' nature as wild things, more animal than human. Look at how they ate, for example, swallowing live fish whole. They could turn anything into a weapon, so we had to stop giving them utensils. A couple of us had wounds to prove it. *You don't know fear until you've had a fork flung at your neck,* someone said, but we rolled our eyes at that. We knew fear.

Their shrieking got in our heads at night, sent us down to the beach without our husbands or children. We shed our clothes and dove in. Bathwater warm, the ocean. Amniotic. Our fingertips touched seaweed. Things flitted, darted, below the surface. We floated naked and didn't make eye contact. Some of us got carried away with each other. Erotic riptides, or what have you. It was not good for our town's stability. All the divorce lawyers lived in the city.

One of us swam out too far and didn't come back. We held a funeral, though we weren't sure she'd died. There was no body. We told our children she'd become a magic dolphin, but our hearts weren't in the story. We wondered if the lost woman had become a mermaid, and secretly, we envied her. Not because we liked the merms. They were an unpleasant bunch, as we've tried to make clear. Just that there was something alluring about the woman's disappearance. Swimming straight out. The unspoken *farewell.*

Our children had their own stories. *She sank like a tank,* they said. *Deep down to the bottom of the ocean.*

Our children were mostly jerks about it.

#

The merms were wild things, we said in town meetings – it became a refrain – and mostly primitive. They hadn't evolved the way we had. It would be like trying to teach a shark to use utensils.

Sharks wouldn't seduce a teenage boy! someone would inevitably yell.

It was true, a few romantic relationships had developed, and the degree of appropriateness of these was unclear, which made our meetings trickier over time. We didn't want to offend anyone. Mothers of teenagers came in weary, haggard, bruised. From what we could gather, the merms weren't any kinder to them or their kids after romance. That was what we called it, *romance,* in deference to the parents, but at least one woman, whispering over coffee refills in the back, gave us the scoop. *It's disgusting,* she said. *I saw them going at it in broad daylight. Poor kid groaning on the pool steps while she gyrated on his lap. He couldn't have got up if he tried. And after? She snarled at him, how they do, and lunged. I heard he got twelve stitches! Did that stop him? No m'am, it did not.*

We talked publically about the problem the merms posed to our sons. We kept talking about our sons, our well-meaning-if-not-entirely-bright sons, until finally, during one poorly-attended meeting, this woman in the middle of the room shouted, *What about our husbands? Where are they? Open your eyes, people!*

A few of us ushered her outside.

We weren't keeping tabs. We didn't need to do headcounts. We looked to the right and to the left, saw what we saw, and went on with our lives.

Besides, who would want to probe the psychology of that? Our husbands came home late, smelling of mint and soap, maybe a faint tang of chlorine, but we didn't ask questions. They kissed us on our foreheads and made elaborate breakfasts and took out the trash. They no longer bothered us with their early-morning erections. They took care of clean-up and stopped coming to meetings. But that was not the point. The point was to figure out how to return our town to normal now that the merms had climbed out of the sea and into our homes.

And that's when it hit us. Homes. They needed their own homes.

Or one home, like an aquarium. We envisioned a huge tank with bubbling treasure chests, some kind of mock shipwreck, an exit that locked. That what we got was more of a bathhouse isn't the point. The point is we tried. Even after the thing with the drowned woman and the divorce lawyers and the teenage boys and maybe some husbands, and the other thing, the one we don't talk about, the thing that happened between *us* in the sea late at night, the point is that even after all that, we still had the merms' best interests in mind.

Our hearts.

Placed perfectly.

Maybe we emphasized the locking exit too much. It wasn't like the merms could escape. We didn't specify who the exits were locking in or out. Locks just seemed like a good idea. We'll admit to averting our eyes when we said that. *Our sons*, we'd say publically, as if that was explanation enough.

We were mostly mothers, or aspiring mothers, so in retrospect it's astounding that we didn't think about the procreative abilities of the merms, but at the time we were distracted with other things, we'll say, we spent all day thinking about what we'd do all night, and we were unwilling to believe most of what people were accusing our men of, and on some level skeptical that it was even possible to impregnate a fish – they were all maids, no males – so call it deluded, but we did not consider what would happen if the merms reproduced. And certainly not what shape those offspring would take, or who would raise them.

It was an oversight, a *grave* oversight, and we take full responsibility, but what's done is done, and groveling won't help.

First we thought it was a problem with the facility, why the merms kept getting sick. The Center for Marine Preservation, as we called it in polite company – known, locally, as The Net – was like a giant bathroom, with a giant saltwater pool in the middle and giant drains all over the floor. Someone more inclined toward ambiance than us put fake banana trees in each corner. A couple of sparrows snuck in and migrated across the ceiling every day. It was nicer than our bathrooms at home, we said. The merms ought to be happy. We felt good about what we'd done. It was beyond humane; it was downright luxurious, especially if you considered how horribly they'd treated us. We hired the janitor from the high school to clean up after them, but they tried to drag him into the water, so he quit. He said it was too big a job for one person, since they were vomiting all over the place, which was news to us, by the way. We didn't know they were sick. But some rookie newscaster got wind of the situation before we could fix it, and then we had a public relations nightmare on our hands, so we hired a SWAT team to make things right. Real SWAT teams are surprisingly expensive, so this was more a gang of out-of-work ex-police officers and security guards. They took what, in retrospect, was an unnecessarily aggressive approach, but the fact of the matter is that once they'd tazed a few of the merms, the rest left them alone.

Not that we approve of what they did. We do not.

We are simply acknowledging that it got the job done.

The merms weren't dumb, just feral. Wild things whose wild had disappeared. Or overheated. In our good moments, we felt bad for them. We imagined them imagining their watery homes, their windswept rocks, their transfixed sailors. We wondered if they missed weightlessness. If there were things you could only think at a certain depth. Did they have fishy friends, marine relatives? Did they cavort with whales? We entered the sea, imagining the land fade away behind us. We held our breath and opened our eyes. We felt for each other – ankles, wrists – found each other – hair skin – took comfort, placed our hearts in our hands. The sea pulled at us, but eventually we muscled back to shore. To our town, which depended on us for its survival.

Some sort of spell, we thought later, how we fell in love with the sea. With what happened in the sea. Sometimes we wonder what would have happened if the merms had stayed, married our husbands, freed us to float all night and day. Sometimes we imagine a world like the merms had, just them and their love for each other, except when, every few hundred years or whatever, they come on land to make babies.

Because, yeah. Turns out we were wrong about the merms. When they left, they returned to the warm ocean just fine.

Took their girl babies with them.

Left us behind with our lovesick sons and philandering husbands. With our guilt and hunger. With all the baby merm boys. With the memory of buoyancy we could never quite shake.

But we're getting ahead of ourselves. We're jumping to the moral because morals are all we have, and while that's perfectly fine with us, it doesn't explain how we got here.

The SWAT team debriefed us at a town meeting in front of several reporters from the city who came to get the scoop on what people were calling Ariel Abuse. *Ariel?* we wanted to say, *get real.* If anything, these were Ursulas, but you couldn't tell the reporters that, and even if you could, it wasn't the real story. The merms were merms. They didn't belong in our cartoons.

Deplorable conditions, the SWAT team said. *Stagnant water. Floating waste and vomit. Skin rashes. Rot.*

We understand your predicament, they said in their warmest SWAT team voices, *but you need a better plan. We are going to have to report this.*

We didn't know who they were going to report it to, but it didn't sound good, and plus the journalists were watching us, so we knew we had to say something. We knew we were going to have to make more promises we knew we couldn't keep. No one understood how hard we'd been trying. People had left our town in droves, or at least what seemed like droves to us. We weren't keeping track. Our losses amounted to more than their numerical value.

That was when one of our husbands who hadn't been at the meeting burst in through the back door and shouted, *They're pregnant! Don't you see? It's morning sickness!* Heads turned. Cameras flashed.

Pregnant merms. We were speechless.

Then we saw our chance.

Of course they're pregnant, we said. *Why do you think we asked for help? These mermaids need prenatal care! They need parenting classes! They need financial resources!*

We had no idea how convincing we were until the checks started rolling in. People love mermaids when they don't have to live with them.

And the convenient thing was, pregnancy subdued the merms. They took to lounging around the pool, holding their growing bellies and combing their hair. They actually seemed to like the new filtration system, the skylights, the tropical gardens. They lost interest in our men, so we stopped locking the doors, even opened them to let in fresh air. Someone's loose puppy fell in the water, and the merms saved it. Birds lit on their fingers. They emitted a smell like honey.

It drove us wild. This was a problem because now our husbands were home at night and noticed when we went out to the ocean. They asked us what we were doing. How long we'd been doing it. They tried to catch us, to extoll the virtues of monogamy, of having another baby. We snuck away; they followed. It was exhausting.

Thank god the merms' gestation period was fairly short.

One night, during a full moon, they all gave birth. Word spread quickly, and we rushed to the Net with supplies: acoustic guitars and receiving blankets, floaty toys, tiny bikini tops. We didn't know what to expect. We gathered around the pool and sang folk songs by candlelight. It was beautiful. Miraculous. The first generation of merms born in captivity. We counted twelve baby girls with tails, twelve baby boys with legs. The merms nuzzled their infants to their breasts. They guided the girls under, placed the boys on the deck. We wept for them and for each other. We rejoiced. Our hearts beat as one. *It has been such a long road*, we said, *but it was worth it to get here.*

The next night, the merms and their girl babies were gone.

The same phone train that had alerted us to the births alerted us to the disappearance. We rushed to the beach, but we were too late. They'd flopped themselves and their babies all the way to the sea. We saw the last merm plunge into the breakers with a baby in her arms. *Goodbye*, one of us called, but the merm didn't look back. We stayed there a long time, thinking about loss, feeling lost. We wondered if it had all been a dream. We wondered if we were crazy. We wondered if we could go back to our lives as they'd been before. We looked at each other and looked at our town and knew that we could.

We wondered what we were going to do with the Net, and that was how we found that all the boy babies had been left behind on the deck.

We didn't even need a meeting to discuss what to do with them. We just picked up the ones that looked most like our husbands or sons, and if there was any debate, sometimes we switched. It was easier to tell who belonged to whom as the boys got older. We found that having the boys was enough closure for most of us.

A few of us grew our hair long and learned how to wail like the merms. The town sex shop filled with tails and seashells.

Our homes became the peaceful sanctuaries we'd always wanted them to be, but we missed each other. A few of us tried to meet up in more ordinary ways; a few of us succeeded. The rest counted love among our losses, and over time, we developed extreme exercise routines and weight-loss regimens that kept our minds off it. We raised the merm boys as our own, soothed their tidal wave nightmares, fed them healthy snacks and sensible dinners, sent them to school with backpacks and mechanical pencils. They grew into bullies and lunatics, but we didn't punish them. We knew the way this needed to end. We fed them and boarded them and when it was time, we turned them out. *Wild things,* we said, *be wild.* We felt a deep satisfaction in watching them go, like we were the ones being freed. We locked our doors and watched them from the windows. They shivered in the night air, waiting to see if we'd change our minds. Then they headed in the direction of the city.

THE PEDESTAL

We put her on a pedestal, a real nice one, not some cheap, plastic shit, but something comfortable – not marble, it was too cold, and not concrete, that was too hard – an ergonomic pedestal made of responsibly-harvested bamboo and recycled bike tires. It stood ten feet off the ground and had an orthopedic shelf where we could put her. She had to stand, there was no way of getting around that. That was the whole point of the pedestal, to put her up where we could see her, hear her, where she could always be available for our worship. She was beautiful, that goes without saying, and she deserved nothing less than our best.

When the pedestal was ready, we hauled it to the park next to the playground because that was a pleasant area of town where the grass was always mowed, far enough from the highway to be quiet but not so far from town that we'd have to fight traffic to get there. The playground, because we were considerate of those of us who had little ones. It was just a few of us at first, but once word spread, the crowd grew. She liked that, we could tell. She'd gone up there willingly, of course – nobody forced anybody, we like to say – but we hadn't been entirely honest about the thing. We'll admit that. We said, Look what we made you! It took us a lot of effort, and we'd be so disappointed if you didn't at least try it out. We pushed her up, and she let us, and then we chanted, Speech! Speech! until she laughed a little, embarrassed, and said, *This is lovely. I can see clear to downtown from here.* We applauded, and she bowed. There was silence while we waited for more. She was so bright, standing up there against the sun. It was perfect. She peered over the side of the pedestal. *So how do I get down?*

We called her different things. Some of her names, like mother, like friend, you'd expect. But once strangers started showing up, they gave her new names, some that couldn't be boiled down to a single word. The-one-into-whom-I-pour-my-nightmares was one. The-architect-of-our-marital-infidelity was another. When we gathered, sometimes we were surprised to see how many new people showed up. Celebrities. Thugs. We didn't know each other. There were a few of us who'd known her from before, but most of us hadn't. Some brought lawn chairs. Some prostrated themselves. We didn't stay long. We had lives, didn't we? Jobs. Hobbies. Shows saved in the queue. Before we left we made sure someone was always there to keep her up.

When she spoke, we wept. We didn't even listen to the words, just ingested her voice. She could say anything – *I'm hungry, I'm bored* – and it was like manna. Yes, we thought. We are all hungry. It's true, we thought. We are all bored. We went home and ate, and paid attention to each bite, concentrated on it, thought about how grateful we were, how each new meal was a gift she'd given us because we wouldn't have noticed it without her, and we were lucky, we were just so goddamn lucky to have found her. And we looked into our boredom, our terrible jobs, our terrible lonely lives, and we found her there, telling us to embrace ourselves in that space, to be present, to breathe, and we did, and it was good.

She grew more beautiful by the day. The redness of her skin deepened until she fairly glowed. And the more her skin changed, the brighter her eyes got. They seemed to float out in front of her. The pedestal wasn't large enough for her to do much, so we savored each movement, how she reached down to scratch a bug bite or shaded her eyes to look over us, past us, beyond us to where the rest of the city buzzed all the way to the horizon. *My children,* she said once. *Where are my children?* We pushed our children forward and threatened them with spankings at home if they didn't cooperate. They all belong to you, we told her, we are all yours. She shook her head. We knelt as one, every person in the crowd, like a miracle, and she lifted her hands over us, raised her face to the sky, and said, *Then you, my children, my flock, let me go. I will be with you always if you set me free.*

But of course we couldn't do that.

We held our breath when she crouched to sleep. A few of the stronger ones gathered around the pedestal to make sure she didn't fall. They held her feet or arms, whatever draped over the edge. Afterward they looked at their hands, the parts of them that'd touched her, and they seemed unable to do anything else for a long time. When they could speak again, they talked of the heat. Her skin, like a furnace. An ember. Their hands carried the heat of her into the city, into their homes. They made love furiously to their husbands and wives. To themselves. The heat passed to whomever they touched, and they breathed her name as they came, felt her there, in their mouths.

Our population swelled until we realized – suddenly, collectively – that we had a problem with equal access. We'd run out of space. The lawn couldn't accommodate our numbers anymore, the playground was blocking half the crowd's view, and several scuffles had erupted over parking. A faction of us staked out territory by pitching tents around the inner circle, and they never left, and that wasn't fair to those of us who had jobs. That, we said firmly, was discrimination. We asked the tent faction to rotate people in, but there wasn't enough time to get to everyone, and some people were all the way in the back, standing in the street. She spoke less and less often, and some of us never got to hear her at all. There was talk of video screens, of microphones, of web-cams. We asked her to say a few more things, for the people who'd missed that last bit. We asked her to speak up. She didn't. We gave her more water, handing up the silver chalice and reveling in the contractions of her neck as she drank. We envied that water. It made us crazy. We said, We understand that you are just one person and we are many, but the whole reason you're up there is so we can see you and hear you, and if we can't see you or hear you or speak to you like the ones in the back can't, then this is not going to work out. We are going to need to change something.

She told us not to move her. If we want to be honest, what she did is she begged us. She'd been up there a long time by now, her hair whipped into delicate knots, salt crystallized on her face. *This is my home now*, she told us. *Can you understand that?* We said we did, but the truth was that we'd gotten off work late, and we'd just had a fight with our spouses, and our children were in trouble again at school, and we'd burnt dinner, and we couldn't get it up, and we needed her to be who she was to us a little more. We needed a lot more, but we were willing to settle for a little. She was so near to perfection by that point – a huge improvement, once she stopped producing solid waste – that a little bit went a long way. At the very least, we needed to be able to see her.

We all chipped in to pay for the new venue. There were enough of us that it didn't take much. Few bucks here and there. Coffee money. We told her, We are taking you to the fairgrounds, isn't that nice? Didn't you once say you liked to go there? We tried to get her to come down and ride in the cab of the truck, but she refused. We think she was afraid we were going to take away the pedestal and dethrone her, and we're not going to say the thought hadn't crossed our minds. Some of us had expressed interest in trying out the pedestal themselves, and a few of us seemed to really be pedestal material. But she wasn't going to give it up. She draped herself over it in this unflattering way, arms and legs spread and gripping the sides, so we picked up the whole thing with her on top and secured it to the truck. She wasn't holding on very tightly. There was some muscle atrophy to work around. She was so thin and red and dry that, as soon as the truck started moving, we feared she might disintegrate in the wind. Honestly, we may have wanted that to happen. It would've been easier to know what to do with her dust, and we considered the kind of ceremony we might have, the covered dishes we'd bring. The memorial we could erect. But we only entertained these thoughts briefly. Because, of course, she was not disintegrating, she was still alive, still there, still upright. It pained her to move her. It wasn't a good look.

But then it was over and there she was, finally, atop the pedestal in the new location, the Main Grandstand, high up on the stage so we could see but not reach her, the pedestal aglow in warm, safe stadium lights. Plenty of space for us in the bleachers. We leaned in. Put our arms around each other. It was a good feeling, what we'd done. A successful transfer. It began to snow. One of us sang this low song, maybe a spiritual, and the sound made us warmer. We thought of peace. We fell in love all over again.

We got a lot of mileage from that moment.

The day she fell was a hard one. We'd let it go on too long, past the point we were comfortable with. One of us should've done it, we knew, brought her down and put her in a home. She was just so damn adamant. *You get the fuck away from me*, she'd say when we hadn't done anything but hand her the chalice. *Mine*, she'd hiss, *mine*. Those were tough times. Many of us stopped coming. By the time she fell, we didn't even fill the bleachers, and a good deal of those who were present were playing games on our phones instead of witnessing her final moment. We heard the gasp and looked up to see the empty pedestal rock back and forth twice, then stop. We took a deep breath. It was the end of something. That much, we knew.

We got up to find her body, to set up the memorial, but she wasn't there. We never found her. Some of us think she shattered on impact; some think she walks among us. We don't say she died, we say she fell. We say she lived, and in so doing, gave us life. We say if we are guilty of anything, it is loving her too much.

At the foot of the empty pedestal, some of us folded our hands. Some looked skyward. Accusations flew. Infighting ensued. The cops had to be called. When the dust cleared, we saw that the pedestal had been pretty badly damaged. That sobered us right up. We got to work repairing it. It would be better this time, we vowed. Safer. More comfortable. We were smarter about this kind of thing now. She'd taught us how to do it right. The new one, we decided, would be built in her honor.

YOU DON'T LIVE HERE

Di proposed to me the night they found her mother in the ravine. She and her mother lived two houses down in a double with stapled-on gutters. Run-down, the kind that used to be nice in the streetcar days. The landlord had thrown out all their stuff for not paying rent, so later, after the EMTs dragged her mother off to Riverside, Di hauled the broken dresser and piles of nighties to my house and threw everything over the metal railing onto my porch.

It snowed, and then the snow melted, and by the time it got warm, all that junk had mildewed, and the stench alone stopped anyone from getting in my door. The cops, maybe. I don't know. Di's mom never came home. After the hospital, she disappeared for two weeks and they found her in a garbage bag in the warehouse dumpster at the end of our street. Between the alley and the train tracks. Couple of detectives interviewed me and I said it was upsetting. I said I lived alone. I said she was a good neighbor, though there weren't any good neighbors there. Just a lot of people scraping by and trying to ignore each other.

#

She was so young. She proposed because we were in love, I guess, but not the kind of love like we wanted to have coffee and babies or share a bank account. I was strong, you understand. I have bulk. I'm thinner now, but back then I was bouncer big. Di, an insect drawn to girth instead of

19

light. Sometimes it seems like she was somebody I watched on TV, one of those tough girls from a crime show, wearing hoop earrings and baggy track pants. But I know she was real because I still have the mirror she proposed with.

"The fuck is this?" I said when she handed it to me. The mirror came in a felt sleeve with the name Allee embossed on it. "Who the hell is Allee?" I said. "And why does she spell her name like an asshole?"

Di laughed. Sometimes she said I was funny. Sometimes she said I was so fucking funny she wanted to stab me in the neck.

So, Allee. I was not Allee. "Aren't you supposed to propose with a ring, or at least something intended for the other person?" I said. "I've heard of plastic rings out of gumball machines, and that's a heartwarming kind of story, people who can't afford the real thing, or who are sentimental about it, you know, because the guy won it for the girl or whatever, or at least paid for it with his own hard-earned quarter, but I've never heard of a mirror. Don't you think that's symbolic? And symbolic of something not good?"

I didn't know what I meant then, and I still don't now. Sometimes when I get nervous I can talk in this really smart way. It's a kind of handed-down intelligence I never earned. My dad was a smart guy. My mom was a bitch, but there you have it.

She laughed, and mad as I was, I can never be mad at somebody laughing at me. I just start to feel shitty.

"Allee's a friend," she said. "You met her." She nodded toward some sweaty girl in a faux fur coat sitting on the couch. She was always having these girlfriends over, and she was fucking a few of them. Maybe the coat wasn't faux. Maybe the girl was just that out of touch.

"I thought you didn't want to be a dyke no more," I said.

"What I want," Di said, "is to marry you. Don't you want to marry me?"

She was lying. She came around when her mom didn't come home because I let her have friends over and watch TV all night, and because I had a decent cable package. And because I pretended not to know when she was fucking that girl. Her mom had told her to find a man who could take care of her, and she did, and that was me. Back then, she'd told her mom that she didn't want a man, didn't need one, and her mom said of course you do, don't be a moron, saying anything different would be dumb, and I know you ain't that. That's one thing I agreed with her mom about. Di wasn't dumb.

"You just want to get your hands on my assets," I said. "You just love me for my services." I didn't really have any assets, except the house, which I'd paid off right after my wife left. I doubted Di knew about that, but I said it all the same. Then I fit the mirror into the sleeve and handed it back to her.

She held her hands in the air, refusing to take it. "I'll drop it," she said. "If it breaks, that's bad luck. Besides, I could say the same thing about you."

"Your bad luck," I said. "What thing?"

"Services," she said.

It was the closest we ever came to talking about what was really going on.

She stared at me. I dropped the mirror, but Allee's sleeve kept it from shattering. We left it on the floor and went to bed. She let me sleep with her sometimes, in the bedroom that used to be mine, and I had to be careful about not putting my hands under the pillows because she slept with knives sometimes. Sometimes not.

I knew things were going well between us when there were no knives under her pillow, and there weren't any that night. She was doing better. And we were not going to get married, but she'd proposed to me, and after a while I let myself feel good about that.

#

I try to go back to this time, live in the moments before everything went to shit. Slow down the good parts. The blush in Di's face, the weight she'd gained clinging to her like the memory of someone else. I don't know who. Not me. Maybe her mom, a flabby woman who had wispy hair that seemed not to move, not even in the wind. She never hurt anyone, not that I knew of. I didn't know who had hurt Di, only that someone had.

Di slept with knives, she said, like her mother's mother before her. They had no need to acquire fear in that family. They were born into it. I'd watched her grow up in this place. I hadn't protected her because you can't save everybody. You do what you can for the ones you love, and I didn't start loving Di until later.

Our neighborhood wasn't really dangerous. We lived in the worst part of an okay neighborhood, off Hudson, where sometimes cars wrecked into the median and sometimes they skidded onto my lawn, but where at least I had a lawn. You know, because a lawn is a sign of prosperity and whatnot. I used to know that kind of shit. I have language, still, for things I no longer understand. Like Di with those knives. She didn't know the real thing that was coming to get her, but she knew, at least, that something was.

#

She said that one time a dead man broke into her bedroom. I asked if it was a ghost, and if so why it couldn't come through the walls, but she said no, it wasn't like that. This guy broke in. Made a bunch of noise. Sat on the edge of her bed whispering things he wanted to do to her. She could see right through him. That was why she didn't call the cops, she said, but her mom was gone and she was underage, and everybody knew what happened if the cops got wind of a situation like that. Nothing good is what. She showed up on my doorstep that evening, and I felt sorry for her, so I let her in. We stayed up all night watching infomercials. She ordered a few things COD. A set of rings. Steak knives. Sent them to my house. By the time they arrived, she was living with me.

"Nothing else happened?" I asked her. "With the dead guy?" This was a long time later. We'd just finished. She was lying on top a pile of laundry, but she didn't have any clothes on.

"You tell me," she said. She pulled one of my wife's crumpled skirts from underneath her. Put her legs through the hole.

"Take that off," I said.

"Why?"

"Just do it."

She took it off. "I'd tell you if anything else had happened."

"You would?"

"Sure," she said. "Sure, I would."

So who knew. Di kept things to herself, and I figured if she wanted to talk about them, she would. And if not? There were plenty of things I was never going to tell her either. Like why my wife's clothes were still on the floor. Di had known my wife and my boys. But we never talked about that.

#

The night she proposed, the ambulance woke us. Di said let's go, like every emergency was hers by definition, so we followed the sound to the ravine. Somebody had dumped her mom in the creek, thrown her right over the edge of the overpass. They were always dumping shit into that creek, toilet bowls and beat-up toys and needles and evidence. There were signs everywhere warning people about the toxicity of the water. That was where they found Di's mom, her back broken, half dead from hypothermia. When the cops asked her what happened, she said she fell. Me and Di knew she'd been thrown. We just didn't know by whom.

"I'm glad she has you," her mom told me in the hospital. Either she had no idea what was really going on between Di and me, or she didn't care. Di was there, and she smiled at me. I didn't know if Di was glad she had me. But she did smile.

While her mom was at Riverside, Di went to the store every night and came home with bottles of fabric softener and ketchup, huge packages of toilet paper, like she was stockpiling for some disaster nobody else knew about. She took the money from my wallet, and I kept replacing it. She said she wanted to do something that suggested permanence. She had a brain on her. She trolled the alleys the way she'd done with her mom, and brought home busted picture frames, candle holders, rain-soaked pillows. More fake plants. Piled everything on my front porch, so pretty soon it looked like I was being evicted. I thought we should try to do things on the up and up, improve our property values and whatnot. But Di was hell bent on trashing the place.

After her mom disappeared, I lugged all that shit to my truck and hauled it to the dump. She was sitting on the porch looking pissed when I got home, but all she said was, "People say a circus train's coming."

"Who says that?" I said.

She pointed at the house next door, the one in between mine and hers, which as far as I knew was vacant. "They do."

We went around back, and lo and behold, don't you know the goddamn circus train came. Our whole street was back there, everybody lined up next to their garbage cans. It was nearly pitch dark, and you couldn't see shit, but you could imagine the lions and seals and whatnot in the closed cars going past, maybe packed in, I don't know, and I kept waiting for the elephant head to be sticking out of one of the cars, ears blowing back in the wind, but it didn't happen. Only real difference was the train had these target-shaped circus logos on the side which you could see in the flash of somebody's camera. And no graffiti. She shook off my hand when I tried to take hers.

"I know you been fucking that girl," I said.

She said nothing.

"You shouldn't do that," I said.

"Don't tell me about should and shouldn't," she said.

The other difference: how slow the train was going. Like it didn't want to disturb the contents.

"Okay," I said. She let me take her hand this time. I thought, We are two people standing in front of a circus train, like in some children's book I never read and never bought for my kids. I think it was chilly, so I might've put my arm around her. That's something I would've done. She wasn't a small person, but she chilled easily. Something about circulation. She said doctors always wanted to test her thyroid. Seemed like everybody was waiting for something to happen to Di, but nobody could agree on what it was going to be.

"You ever been to the circus?" she said.

"Nobody's ever been to the circus," I said. She smiled, so I kept going. "There's never been a ringleader or a bear balancing on a ball, and there sure as hell ain't any tightrope walkers. You ever heard of an actual circus? You ever seen a commercial for one?" She shook her head, squinting up at me. I'd meant to make her laugh, but now I felt like an asshole. She half-believed me.

"I've been to one," she said. "I saw the trapeze."

"No such thing," I said.

"I saw the tooth fairy riding a giraffe," she said. "She had all these teeth."

"And you know what's the real bullshit?" I said. "Human cannonball."

"I saw that, too." Di laughed. "Except it was the Easter Bunny."

"And he landed on a fat-ass unicorn," I said.

Di held my hand in a way that suggested she'd forgiven me. I didn't want her to. I was never going to marry her. We were never going to be family. We'd never be anything more than neighbors.

"He did," she said. "He landed on a unicorn, just like you said. You were there."

"I saw you," I said. "You were a little kid." I felt bad when I said that. I'd known her when she was a little kid. She was still so young.

"But I was happy," she said. "Right?"

"Jesus." I didn't know what to say. "Yes."

The train ended. She started to go back inside. "Wait," I said. "See that?" The last car was going by slowly. It passed. There was nothing left to see. "The elephant. Did you see it? Motherfucker's trunk sticking all the way out. Ears blowing back in the wind."

She didn't smile or nod. "Come inside," she said. "I don't like you lurking behind the house."

It was my house. My yard to lurk in if I wanted. But I went inside. That was just the kind of thing I did for her.

#

When I think of what happened to Di, I think of all the stories I've heard about kids getting smashed by trains, the games of chicken and ghost played on the tracks. So many deaths the high schools started showing these safety videos with kids who looked nothing like Di and her friends, talking about the importance of stopping for the signal. Every time a teen got hit, it was big news. Not like finding somebody's mom in the dumpster. Nobody cared about that. When I heard about Di, first I was relieved. I thought, At least she got away. From me. From this neighborhood with its dead men and circus trains. She had my knives on her. Nobody told me that, but I knew. I knew it like I knew why she saved her mom's shit. There are some weapons you can't give up, not even after the fight's all done.

#

The rest blurs together. I'm older now, certifiably old, and I go around saying things like, "My memory isn't what it used to be," which is a lie and also is the truth, because my memory never used to be great. I say, "I forget things," which is true, and after I've said it, I say it again because I've forgotten. My grandmother had Alzheimer's, and when my brother and I visited she'd smile and ask what we did for a living. We were both in high school. It didn't matter what shit we made up – I'm batting for the Reds, Grandma! – because she'd smile and ask again a minute later. I don't have Alzheimer's. It's more like my memory has cracked apart and the pieces are crawling away from each other. I can get them together if I try, but I don't try. I only want to remember when Di proposed. How she always smelled sweet, even after hauling shit out of the alley. Di never sweated, and she was proud of that, you know, like people who get cocky over the fact that their kids got teeth early or something, like it means their kids are genius teeth growers. My wife was like that. My kids got early teeth.

I don't think it's Alzheimer's, but I guess Alzheimer's people don't think it's that, either.

#

She didn't stop fucking that girl, the one in the fur coat. Allee. Once I caught them in my bedroom. I watched for a while, getting pissed and hard at the same time, and then I pulled the girl off Di and told her to take her goddamn coat and leave. Then I told her, On second thought, stand right here. Di started to get dressed, but I pushed her back onto the bed. She said, "Why don't you just lay off, you idiot?" so I smacked her. The girl in the fur coat started crying, even though I'd only smacked Di on the cheek, not hard enough to leave a mark, and it wasn't like she was a girl who'd never been hit. Still. I don't like to think about it. But that's the trouble: you try hard enough to forget, you might succeed. Then you're left with the guilt of what you may or may not have done compounded by the emptiness of not being sure.

So I sit now in the moment before she spoke, let her words sink a little more softly into her mouth, her mouth pouting up at me, her look like she was about to say something sweet.

"Why don't you just lay down?" That was the kind of thing she could've said. Then someone laughed, maybe the girl in the coat. Maybe it was me. Maybe I laughed because I thought I was supposed to, because she was being cute on purpose. It might not have been funny. I don't know.

Maybe she was the one laughing at me, and I hit her for being a bitch.

"What the fuck, Brain?" she said, holding her mouth like her jaw might fall off. Then she reached over to the bedside table, grabbed her keys, and whacked me in the head with them until I got off her. My name isn't Brain. That was what she called me when she wanted to make me feel bad, as in The Brain, as in, I didn't have one. She was young enough to think that was funny. Old enough to know better. Old enough to know the kinds of things she knew, like how to fix toilets and give good blow jobs. How to con old men out of their property. How to make all those kids she brought into my house feel like it was their own. Sometimes that was nice, like a Thanksgiving that never ended. Mostly it sucked.

She called me Brain and hit me with her keys and I started bleeding from my scalp. I took the keys back and told her to get out.

"Give me back my keys," she said.

"You want me?" I said. "You love me?"

"Yes," she said. "You know I do. Baby. Darling. Cupcake."

"You called me an idiot," I said.

"You are an idiot," she said. But she made it sound nice this time, like in the way the whole world was idiots, not just an old man in love with a teenager. "You are my idiot," she said.

How she could make that sound sweet, I don't know.

"You calling me your possession?" I said.

"I am."

"You saying I have to do anything you tell me?"

"I am," she said. "Give me my keys."

I did. I thought we were going to have sex after that, but we didn't.

She said, "Sometimes I feel bad about this. If you want to, you can kick me out. You can." She held the keys in her fist. "You just can't push me around. It isn't right."

"I know," I said. "I'm sorry."

"It makes everything sadder," she said.

"I'm sorry," I said again.

She started to cry. It was an odd thing. She didn't usually cry about anything. I was afraid if she started having emotions like that, she'd leave me. That is my confession. I'm not proud of it.

"Everything," she said, and stopped. She looked around the room – my bedroom, her bedroom, our bedroom – like the light had changed. The girl with the fur coat was sitting in the corner like she was used to being punished. "This is so fucked up," Di said.

"What is?" I said.

"Nothing." She went downstairs to the kitchen to stare into the fridge. I should've followed her, but instead I went out back and hammered the shit out of a loose board on the fence. By the time I went inside, Di had more people over and everything was normal again.

#

I wanted her to stop me. I kept buying her knives, and she kept taking them. I had to switch up the stores where I bought them because I was getting funny looks from the cashiers. They were just kitchen knives. But still. You could see the question on their clerks' faces: what does he do with all of them?

I gave them to Di. I thought, if she tries to kill herself, I am definitely going to kick her out.

It was my turn to go, not hers. I was the one in trouble. I told her I'd put her in my will, that she'd be taken care of if anything happened to me. *Anything*, I said meaningfully. I went upstairs to her, which I had no business doing. She had those knives, and I figured one day she'd use them. She could've. She had the know-how. The opportunity. Maybe she really did love me. Maybe she thought it was worse punishment to let me live knowing what I'd done. What I was still doing. I felt bad, she was right about that. But not bad enough to quit.

"I'm coming up," I'd shout from the bottom of the stairs.

She wouldn't say anything.

"I'm halfway up," I'd say when I was.

When I got to the bedroom, she'd say, "Ask not for whom the bell tolls." Something she must've picked up at school.

"I won't," I'd say. Then I'd crawl up into her and forget who I was.

#

The last time I saw her, she was stepping between stopped train cars. She hopped onto the coupler and stood for a minute, looking out at where she was going. Beyond the track was the interstate, headlights winking around the curve, and beyond that, a hardware store and a Dollar General and a tire place. She looked out on all this, but I couldn't see her face so I didn't know if she was sad or hopeful or what. What I saw was more bullshit she could help me forget. I'd worked in the lumberyard at that hardware store before my wife left. She didn't take any of her stuff with her, and I didn't get rid of it because I kept thinking she'd come back. After that I didn't willingly come out of my house again until Di moved in. I let the pipes freeze in the winter. Let the yard grow up in the summer. Nobody seemed to care, but then somebody must've called someone because the city came out and put a notice about the lawn on my door. So I mowed it.

Not long after that, Di showed up on my doorstep like the reincarnation of a memory I'd tried to suffocate.

I watched her watch the neighborhood from between those train cars. When the train started to move, she hopped down on the other side. She looked back at the house, almost right at me. We watched each other like that for a while. I wondered if she wished I would suffocate her.

When she got back to the house, I was still in the yard. She stood behind me. "Marry me," she said. "Do the right thing for once in your life."

"Give it a rest," I said. "There's no such thing as a right thing." I didn't turn around. I should've turned around. I know that now.

"Yes, there is," she said. "You'll see. You'll regret it if you don't do it."

"Make me," I said.

She went back inside and I never saw her again.

They said it was an accident. They said she didn't suffer. They didn't tell me that, but I knew they said it because that was the kind of thing people said, and also because there was a blurb about it in the newspaper. It happens a lot around here. Kids trying to beat the trains. Maybe Di got the idea from the safety video at school. The girl in the fur coat was with her, but she got out of the car in time.

It was several days after the collision that I heard about it. I thought she and the girl had run off together. There were several days when I was worried she'd come back. There were several more when I hoped she would.

#

I recognized the girl because of her coat. I hadn't seen her since I pulled her off Di that night. This was a long time later, but she was still wearing the same coat. I didn't know her last name. I didn't want to know it. I was just trying to be close to Di again, you know? I was driving home from this bar and I saw the girl waiting for the bus, and maybe it was the beer, but I didn't even think about it. I just stopped. Told her I'd take her to Dairy Queen. I don't know why she got in the car with me, except that maybe she missed Di, too.

The Dairy Queen on the corner had a drive-thru, and that's where I took her. She got a Snickers Blizzard. Then I drove to the opposite side of the train tracks, directly across from my house. The sweaty smell of her filled the car. I left the headlights on. I watched her cry while she pried the lid off the Blizzard and wedged in the plastic spoon. She ate the whole fucking thing. She never even offered me a bite. I guess she was pretending I wasn't going to do what she knew I was going to do because she kept pinching her coat together at the neck and shivering.

"Ouch," she said once, touching her temple. She had ice cream in the corner of her mouth, but when she licked it, her tongue just pushed the drip further down. Everything about her was sloppy: her blonde hair, her broad lips. Not fat, exactly. Well-sugared.

It's not that I was scared that night with the girl in the fur coat. I wasn't nervous. But Di was my last. There was no replacing her. I gave that girl a good hard try, but it was no use, so finally I just hauled her out of my truck. I told her to go home and not to accept rides from strange men anymore. She left crying like an idiot about her coat, which was still in my truck, how it was cold and she had such a long walk home to the suburbs. I told the girl to quit crying. "When you freeze to death," I said, "you'll feel warm."

That made her cry harder, but at least she left. I put on her coat. I wasn't wearing any clothes underneath it. Maybe I was hoping to freeze to death. I thought maybe I'd hop a train, but I'd never tried it before, so I didn't know how. It seemed like something people did, hobos and whatnot, riding the rails, so I figured it couldn't be that hard. But I was wrong. Or in the wrong spot. The trains went too fast even when they seemed slow. Confused, they called me later. Senile. It wasn't true. I knew where my clothes were. I knew how to put them on.

#

When it became clear I wasn't going to hop any trains, I faced my house. There wasn't anything left for me there, no reason to stay with a bunch of land-grabbing high school kids who didn't seem bothered in the least by Di's death. I hadn't stood back there since the circus train, and I couldn't figure out why it looked different until I noticed the fence. Then I saw it. My name, spray-painted over and over. Not my name. The name she called me. Brain. I walked toward the fence, though my legs felt weak, and the closer I got, the more I saw. Words carved into the wood. Written in marker in Di's handwriting. Messages I'd never seen, a wall of language from top to bottom, things she'd said to me and things she'd never said to me. I fell to my knees. Brain. Braindead. Brain Dead, two words. I'm sorry, Brain.

I love you. I hate you.

Marry me, Brain.

You'll be sorry.

"You fucking bitch," I said, but I was crying.

I guess I was getting real cold by then. There was a bunch of trash back there, and some of it was Di's. Or it could've been. I followed it to the dumpster where they found her mom, and inside it, I found more of her things. Evidence that she'd been here. Or that someone had. I stumbled into some hoboes living back there, and they tried to make me leave. I don't know who finally called the cops but two of them showed up. I told them I had evidence of foul play, and they laughed.

"Look at my fence," I said. "It's a crime scene."

"What, that graffiti?" they said.

I was trying to tell the truth, but it was too late. They asked me where I lived, and I told them I was homeless. They asked about my relatives, and I told them about Di.

"Di what?" one of the cops said.

"I don't know."

"This is your wife?"

"My wife ran off," I said, "because I wouldn't marry her."

The cops thought that was hilarious. I was furious. They were trying to trick me, pretending to care the way people do.

Things slid. A girl came out of my back door, one of Di's old friends who wouldn't leave. "That girl is trespassing on my property," I said, but the cops didn't seem to care.

"That's your daughter," one of them said. Maybe there was only one. Maybe the other one had already left.

"I have a wife and two sons," I said. I didn't know how we'd gotten to the patrol car, but there we were. He was in the front seat. Maybe it was an ambulance.

"Your wife's dead," the cop said. "That's what your daughter said."

"Wrong wife," I said.

"What's that?" He said it like he didn't care. Like we'd been through all this before, and maybe we had. I had a blanket around me that I kept trying to throw off.

"Where am I?" I said, and he said, "Settle down."

"We are not understanding each other," I said. "She was lying. She's not my daughter. I want to go home."

"Sure," the cop said. "Tell me where you live."

That made me mad. Really mad. He knew I couldn't answer that.

"She left me," I said. "I just wanted to tell her fuck you for doing that."

He laughed. "I hope I end up as feisty as you."

I didn't know what that was supposed to mean, but I knew it wasn't a compliment. This cop was the worst kind of human being.

"You got any other family?" he said.

"No."

"Anybody we can call?"

"No."

"You understand why I'm asking you?"

"Yes," I said.

We were in the place now. I lost track of one moment by trying to figure out another. I realized I was old. I realized I didn't know how long this had been happening. Then I forgot again.

"Here," the cop said. I was losing language, and I couldn't figure out what he was handing me. It was a cup of coffee, but I didn't know what to do with it.

"Home," I said, but it didn't come out sounding like any word I knew. "I think I'm having a stroke," I said, "or maybe a stroke is having me." I was making a joke, but no one laughed.

I collapsed, and they took me to the hospital. I came to before we got there, and I realized again that I was old. That I was dying. Then I forgot it again. I thought I was back in the cop car. "You taking me in, boys?" I said. "That it for me?"

"Hush, Brain," Di said.

"Are you a ghost?" I asked her. I could see her standing over me.

"You're the ghost," she said. "You're the dead man."

I didn't know if that was true or not, but it could've been, so I apologized. I told her how I tried to stop time, to live in the moment when she proposed. I told her that time can stand still or it can race, and that sometimes you think one thing is happening when it isn't. I say these things about time, and the guy in my room, the one who works here, says, "You're pretty deep, aren't you?"

"The point is," I tell him, "I want to go home. And they won't let me."

"Man, this here's your home," he says.

"I'm saying that I want it back. My house. My life. I want her out of it."

"Come on, now," the guy says. "You said you loved her."

"You don't understand. She wasn't capable of love." I am heartbroken still. Or all over again. I am orbiting the heartbreak, waiting for it to pull me in. I don't tell the guy how old Di was.

"You don't believe that," the guy says.

"You're right," I say. She loved me, in a way. It was a kind of love. It was a piece of me.

She could've called the cops. She could've pressed charges. She could've used the knives. She could've run away.

"I just want to go home," I say.

I don't know what I'm referring to anymore. This is what we say here, what we all say all the time. We know it's important to keep saying it. We know we've given up something huge.

The guy looks at me with real sadness, the way the people who work here never do. Maybe I just wish he would.

"I know, buddy," he says.

He leads me from the toilet to the easy chair. He is kind to me. I sit on the chair with my feet propped up, feeling what I feel, knowing what I know, which is that I had a good life. My mind tries to wipe the thought away, but if I concentrate I can hold onto it a minute longer. And that minute becomes the next one. And the next.

A good life. That's what I have.

THE STEPMOTHERS

The stepmothers are knocking. They have reached the porch and are pounding on the screen door, grocery bags slack with rain, junk mail decomposing in their arms, phones buzzing, hair dripping. Shoes much too tight. They are fumbling with purses and kicking the doors, cursing leaky gutters, alert to what's gathering in the trees. Is that thunder? Are those birds? Across the city, the stepmothers are locked out and defenseless. They are fuming and anxious. They are almost home. They are a single continuous action.

Ask them, What is the most dangerous creature?

They will reply, Stepchildren.

The children are holding the doors shut. The children with their glassed-in laughter, their nocturnal urges, their dexterity with locks. The children always breaking and entering, always alone in the forest for no reason. Children mocking the stepmothers through the windows, doing the thing where they mouth the stepmothers' words in slo-mo: *Op-en uh-up!*

The stepmothers want to fill those mouths with lethal fruitflesh, poison apples the unnecessary old story, the genetically modified stuff in the supermarket good enough these days. These days, eradication is slow but requires no extra steps. They don't buy organic or keep the raw meat separate. They microwave in bowls clearly marked Do Not Microwave. They aerosol everything, leave the water running, litter and burn Styrofoam. They know better, these days, than to slam a child's head in a freezer. Their revenge is a long con.

They throw their plastics right into the trash.

They slice unwashed apples and eat all the meat themselves.

Ask them, Revenge for what?

They will reply, We never sought redemption.

#

The stepmothers are knocking. The rain is not worsening with their anguish because they are not really part of this world. They are incompletely drawn, unconnected to anything but plot. They have no mothers, were born into stepmotherhood and trained to make mistakes. They have undiagnosed personality disorders and repressed trauma. They have bad debt. They never finished rehab or high school. Their only friends are mirrors and ovens.

They were raised on the same stories everyone was, and of course each stepmother had hoped to grow into a princess, or an only daughter, or a woodsman, or a godmother. But the evidence of her nature was always there. The widow's peak. The flawless skin. The early puberty and unnatural cravings. The way songbirds didn't light on their fingers so much as go for their eyes.

Ask them, When did you first know?

They will reply, Who among you can't be convicted of cruelty?

The stepmothers never felt the tidal pull of maternity, never consented to age, never gave away their bodies. Not to children, not to husbands, not to science or time. The story is greed, the story is vanity, but the truth is that they all married the same wrong guy. The one with the kids he never mentioned, and the kingdom he said practically ran itself, and the good job he swore he wasn't *right about to lose.* He was handsome and simple and easy to love. He proposed the same way to all of them, rich and poor, beautiful and wicked: *Wanna?* The stepmothers, all on their third glasses of wine, hoping they were part of a different story: *I do!* And then the blunt reality, the hateful children and idolized first wife, the kingdom that monopolized his schedule, the job he lost in the time it took for the marriage to become legal.

The truth is that everybody knew what the stepmothers were doing to those kids and nobody stopped them. They were nothing if not watched. Don't say you didn't know how this would end. If the question is stepmother, the answer is always doom. They are repeat offenders. Lost causes. They never save anyone, and are never, themselves, saved. They are climaxes, the only resolution to which is death.

Ask them, What haunts your dreams?

They will reply, The falling action.

#

The stepmothers are knocking, but now the action is perfunctory. They get where this is going. They will not be reduced to begging, won't cajole these children who don't love them. They give the children an ounce of begrudging respect for evading the cookpot. It's there, on the stove inside, the stepmothers' most prized possession. You know how it is with stepmothers, always cooking what isn't food. They look at the children and think, What a meal you would make. They send their last texts before their phones die: *There's meat in the fridge for dinner.*

Don't ask about the meat.

The stepmothers stop knocking. They watch the trees, knowing what they know about the birds. Knowing that other ways of getting inside won't work. If they try to smash the windows with rocks, upon touch the rocks will turn into bread dough or bubbles or birds with shattered skulls that no one will believe the stepmothers didn't murder. The birds tell every other story. They tease, waiting for the stepmothers to try a new twist. The trees are as full of feathers as they are of leaves. They have the eyes of lost children. *You don't understand*, the stepmothers want to tell them. *It didn't use to be so terrible to lose a child.*

It used to be common.

It used to be necessary.

But you cannot tell a dead thing its life was an obligation, or a tax, or a disaster. Women used to die in childbirth, too, which is how the stepmothers came to be. The birth moms are always dead when the story begins.

Ask them, What will you teach us?

They will reply, To finish what you start.

They have no stretch marks or scars, but they are much older than they appear. They will not go quietly. They will die, but they are never victims. Never burdens. Their deaths restore order. Keep good on the side of good so that commercials and religion and fashion magazines will continue to be effective. So that women can keep giving birth to happily ever afters.

Which is not the whole story. You know it's not. It is great luck to be a stepmother because it means your tale will be told. The stepmothers fidget on the stoops: some have secrets. Some of their stepchildren look uncannily like them. Same arched eyebrows. Same swishy gait. It doesn't mean the stepmothers didn't hunger for them just the same.

Ask them, Why did you lie?

They will reply, We're still here, aren't we?

#

The birds are coming for the stepmothers. They will lure the stepmothers into traffic and over cliffs. In the yard, the stepmothers' groceries have broken through the bags, and on the lawn are the ingredients to a meal they will never make. They drop their other belongings and shake out their hair, exactly like every princess. They look through the window at the laughing boy children and think, You will never become a stepmother.

They look at the girl children and think, You don't even know you've been poisoned.

The air is thickening with bird dander; the stepmothers begin to itch. This is their last chance to exit the stoop. To do things they've never been allowed to do, like floor a minivan out of the lot, or roller skate, or spend all day browsing in a record store. This is the unnarrated interim. The white space. This is heaven for stepmothers. No one knows what they will do because no one is watching. For all we know, they've already gone splat.

Ask them, What words do you want on your gravestone?

They will reply, Just get it over with.

So the children are alone now, and triumphant. And free. They have retained their purity and their paternity and their inheritance. They have their whole lives ahead of them. They have spent only a leaf or two of their innocence – a bargain – in exchange for the future that the stepmothers were denied. They high five and say it was so easy, like taking candy from a stepmother. The children are good, so good they barely mourn the loss of her, though she finds them, of course, after the story ends. The story never ends where we're told it ends. The children cease to be children. They will be at the stove one day, reaching for the bubbling pot, when they'll hear a knocking. Turn to see a bird at the door. Remember that *she* told them never to let a bird in the house. That *she* always seemed overly concerned about the birds.

The bird will ask, Where are the children?

The children will look around, unsure what this means. Suddenly aware of the quiet, the emptiness of their homes. Did they grow up and lose children of their own? Did they eat them? They will be struck by the feeling that they are missing something. That the moral of the story is not what they thought it was.

They will answer, They were here just a minute ago.

DEAR FAIRY GODMOTHER

1.

I'm tired of crashing balls in borrowed gowns. I'm tired of prohibitive return policies. I can no longer forgive the atrocities in my story. Do you suggest I ignore the blood in my shoes? Can we look at this through a Marxist lens? I don't know why the night must end on a single cold foot.

2.

I don't think this pumpkin is working. My dress is wrecked. My prince is gone. Transformation has ruined the mice. They spend their days researching spells and creating online profiles. PonyPride17. RestlessRider. I don't know where they found the Ouija board, but I've told them you're no ghost. Your alchemy resists duplication. None of us comprehend your rules, so arbitrary and persnickety, so clearly intended as obstructions. The mice refuse to believe that the best part of life is behind them. They hold out hope: if it happened once. If we could spin the circumstances right, acquire credit, purchase the magic words that would conjure you again. If midnight was more metaphor than expiration date.

3.

Are your terms negotiable? I'd take an ounce of self-respect over a footman any day. Or, if you want that I should flee the prince, surely there are better reasons to do so than a curfew. Let's say, instead, that my regalia begins to grate. It's so stiff, so cumbersome, so devoted to its own shape. Let's say that all evening I've wished to shed my gown, snakelike, and consume it. Fashion me a suit of ash in its place; the slinkiest armor the kingdom has ever seen. This time, I'll wear body paint and pasties, a strap-on beard, high-tops. Let's face it: I'm as suited to the throne as the mice are to saddles. I'd rather slay another prince than marry one. Royalty is just a respectable form of servitude.

4.

I'm tired of not being on television. I'm tired of talking to princes who tactfully pause before asking about my past. Every prince is expert at something: the one who only talked about fracking. The one who only talked about saltwater aquariums. "No one has breadth anymore," I tell the mice. "All they care about is their own tiny kingdom."

The mice are sensitive to my derogatory use of the word *tiny*.

"Maybe you're bad at conversation," they say.

"You're not even supposed to be able to talk," I say.

They remind me that logic has not distracted my story for two hundred years.

Touché.

I'm tired of stepmother apologists with their unconventional points of view. I'm tired of romantic montages and tragic backstories. Give me a guy with a day job. Someone who's strategic about the carpool lane. Anyone can go to charm school; give me the dropout who can hold his liquor. The one who will remind me that horses are glorified rodents.

I'm tired of needlework. Of inhibitions and censorship. I'm tired of not dropping F-bombs around children just to see their mothers wince. I'm tired of not doing shots out of glass slippers every night.

5.

You realize, of course, that there are more interesting objects to make out of glass. A wig, a codpiece, a prosthetic heel. I think of them at odd times, my stepsisters. My sisters from another mother, my antagonists, my straw-man lady friends. Thrown in the mass grave of characters who exist solely to be punished. Have you ever felt like that? Have I gone too far? Consider what you'd do: some chick mutilates her own foot to fit the shoe you're holding. Am I naive to think someone should've reached for a tourniquet? The moral of the story is that people can be cruel. The mice would like to know if people are ever anything *but* cruel. *Not like horses,* they say. *Now there's a superior species.*

Can we all just admit that there are things we'd cut off body parts to get? Don't tell me this was their punishment. Gift me with the courage to follow in their steps.

6.

The mice persist in running around half-naked. They ate three of their own babies, but no telling if it was a crime of passion or opportunity. They gnaw inspirational messages into the pumpkins. I tell them they are too sentient to go around without pants. They reply it is a shame about my gown.

"I'm not wearing a gown," I say.

"That's what we mean," they say. "You could put in a little effort."

It's too hard to comb my hair these days, let alone change my shirt. The prince and I were together long enough for the world to change, and change again, and make itself unrecognizable to the girl I used to be. Now I survive off alimony and royalties. I've developed night sweats, which the mice insist is a side effect of depression and metacognition. My gynecologist says I'm pre-menopausal. I say I'm also pre-married and pre-pregnant and pre-dead. He says I have a perfect cervix, and I consider adding that to my online dating profile. But I don't because the mice wrote my profile and will be pissed if I change it. They called me a social climber and a good catch.

For employment, they put *service industry*.

For religion, *realist*.

Looking for: *human (preferred)*.

They gave my shoe and cup size in lieu of height and weight. They didn't mention the condition of my house or any of my medications.

7.

Screw the gown, lady, give me new skin. Ostrich feathers, whale blubber, a pelt cobbled from predators. Give me milky eyes and accessory organs. Retractable claws. Give me scutes and a second row of teeth. When the clock strikes, I'll hatch. Grow to the size of my container. Sprout feet from vestigial feet.

8.

Sorry. I fear my crassness has kept you away. I could blame the mice for procuring a thirty-dollar bottle of wine last night, but the truth is I've hardened on my own. I've become critical, demanding. I've lost faith in humanity but can't reconcile myself to being alone. I've unfriended the prince and most of the kingdom, and the only messages I get are from anonymous fans that are probably the mice.

This is all to say: I don't need a gown. The pumpkins are ruined, but I'll take any vehicle.

If it would be easier, I could throw the next ball. We could make it a bona fide Freak Show, display oddities instead of formal wear. What gift would you give me then? I knew a woman who claimed she could orgasm at will, but I'd rather be taken by surprise. Program me to climax to particular things that I wouldn't know in advance. A man eating hash browns, say. One-and-a-half line spacing. Broken finish lines. The word *irregardless.* The word *kerfuffle.* Air horns. Irony. Pumpkin spice. I'd encounter some right away; others I never would. But the possibility of enrapture would always be there, attainable only in discrete units.

The mice say I have too much time on my hands. I say I'm bored by anyone who's not talking about mortal sin. I want us all to wear greed on the outside where everyone can see it.

This is the condition of remorse. I'm going to invite Orgasm Woman to my ball and put her under lights. Come one, come all.

9.

This was much easier the first time.

10.

The mice still want to believe that we're the chosen ones. Even now, we speak from the vantage point of the lucky. Consider the girl who never escaped her stepmother's house. She had a fairy godfather, a real lecherous sort. When he found her crouching in the fireplace, sorting lentils from ash, he didn't ask permission to take what she hadn't offered. She had a child made of glass that she dressed in rubber. No precaution was too much. When the child cried, her tears shattered. She needed to be kept very warm.

The glass girl obsessed over other people's pain because she could feel none herself. She became expert at invoking it, her mother the easiest target. She'd ask about her mother's childhood, then say, "At least you weren't made of glass." It was so easy.

Consider the doves that pecked out the stepsisters' eyes. They didn't need the provocation of rabies or habitat loss. We're meant to accept their aggression as fair punishment for the wicked.

Consider the taste of the eyes. It's not a meal that would sit well.

Consider the debilitating sense of entitlement you'd get from having your wishes granted and foes vanquished.

Consider that *no one in the whole kingdom shared my shoe size.* Can we just pause over that?

Consider the prince who contacted me after a week of no contact to tell me he wouldn't be contacting me anymore. In the chronology of the relationship, his message was such an anomaly that I couldn't help responding.

I said: *Send this text a week ago.*

He said: *This is why you're single.*

I said: *I thought you said you weren't contacting me anymore.*

He said: *That's mature.*

I said: *Thanks, Prince Obvious.*

Prince Redundant.

Prince Pointless.

No one's paying me to be mature, and frankly, I don't see the benefit. No one's ever said, *I love her maturity.*

The glass girl knows that if she demands candy from the kids at lunch, they'll give it to her because otherwise she'll threaten to break herself and blame it on them. When she gets older, she'll carry glass condoms in her purse; older still, she'll store glass dentures in a glass of water by her bed. She'll never get a piercing or a sunburn or a sore throat. To her dying day, she'll insist on comfortable shoes.

I'm tired of not being the glass girl.

11.

The mice have acquired some kind of horse skin. They know something I don't about agency.

But I know something they don't about dramatic irony.

12.

The prince who said he wasn't contacting me anymore contacted me to ask if I wanted to hang out again. The mice are too preoccupied with their horse skin to care. It smells like a slaughterhouse, but they stay up stitching and buttonholing and oiling it all night.

I agreed to meet Prince Pointless for Happy Hour, then stood him up.

13.

The ex-hubs sent the Grand Duke to check on me. He does this every so often because he's old school like that, refuses to upgrade to wireless or BluRay. He calls cell phones "mobiles" and uses a fax machine. But the Grand Duke and I always got along. He gives me the scoop on the string of princesses my ex- has moved through, predictably young and blonde, how he tired of them and has since taken to random hook-ups from craigslist ads the Duke prints out. It takes a while for the Duke to ask about the smell, and right after he does, like they've been granted permission, the mice come out in the horse skin. You can tell they're trying to be convincing, pawing at the carpet and making these high-pitched whinnies, but the seams are showing and the body is lumpy and they've glued craft-store googly eyes to the empty sockets. You wouldn't think it'd be possible to make a horse skin look creepier than it already does, but those eyes do the trick.

"Dude," the Duke whispers. "That's effed up."

"And they wonder why I never bring anyone home," I say.

The mice complete a slow circle of the living room, showing off their handiwork, then disappear into a back bedroom. We hear them arguing. The Duke turns to me.

"Look." He puts a hand on my shoulder. "The Prince – he's a wreck. And by the looks of it, you're not doing so hot yourself. I'm going to tell you what I told him: everybody thinks *happily ever after* is a crock, but it's not. It's real. It's possible. But you have to keep reinventing it, like everything else. You have to figure out different ways to perform it. Balls are ridiculous pageantry, I know, but they serve a purpose."

"That's what she said," I say.

He ignores me. "They remind us that happiness is the interior realization of the external presentation. Not the other way around."

"You should tell that to the mice," I say. "They love inspirational speeches."

"Dress for the ending you want," he says. "Fake it 'til you make it."

"You're saying I should wear the gown."

"I'm saying," the Duke says, "that the mice have the right idea. Poor execution, but the right idea."

We hug. After he's gone, I cry for a long time. I don't know what to wear because I don't know who I want to be.
14.

I fill out a personal ad on craigslist. I call myself a reformed protagonist and describe, precisely, the kind of sex I know the prince likes. I wait for his call.

15.

The first few years we were together, I never expressed a single demand of my own. My marriage felt so fragile, so whimsical: what the fairy godmother giveth, the fairy godmother could taketh away. Later, a therapist told me it wasn't uncommon for trauma to follow in a fairy godmother's wake. It wasn't something anyone talked about, but the whole process of first receiving, then losing, your heart's desires – especially all in the course of one night – was bound to fuck you up long-term. That wasn't what the therapist said. The therapist said I needed to *process* and *work through* it. I needed to express to the prince my fears, my doubts, my desires. Cross-class relationships were challenging, the therapist said. The prince might never fully understand where I'd come from.

He'd never asked where I'd come from.

He didn't know how I searched for my stepsisters, how I tracked them to this assisted living place where the trail went cold. How I'd planned, when I saw them, to ask if they'd let me record them. *Start at the beginning*, I'd have said. *Tell me where you're from.*

I told the therapist I was tired. Just so tired. The therapist said it would only get worse, and I said it was my impression that therapists weren't supposed to say things like that.

Eventually the prince and I stopped having sex. From what I gather, it's not uncommon. The thing he wanted most was for me to own my desires. To wear my body like a piece of jewelry. Give him the gift of my appetite.

But I owned nothing outright. You, the mice, the kingdom were keeping tabs. The glass slipper glowed red as eyes in the night.

16.

I wear a costume to the castle and ride the second iteration of the horse-skin horse. Our progress is painfully slow. I have lots of time to reconsider. I visualize possible scenarios: he recognizes me at once and sends me away; he recognizes me and is into it; he doesn't recognize me but passes on the opportunity; he doesn't recognize me and falls in love; and on and on, while the mice drag clip to its blessed clop. The doves, true to character, sing their bitchy rhymes. *Roo coo kite, that horse ain't right. Roo coo creak, the prince is gonna freak.*

I've tried to take the Duke's words to heart, so I opted for a leopard-print, halter-top catsuit. Thirty-five bucks and free shipping, plus another fifty for the jeweled mask. The shoes I already had.

Not those shoes.

I wonder if you, fairy godmother, will appear en route, wave your wand to turn the horse skin into a stretch limo and my love handles into perkier tits. But of course you don't. It takes us three hours to get across town, but we make it to the castle on our own, our patched-together caravan of sweat and hope.

We're routed to the back entrance, as if the paparazzi can be deterred that easily, and I tie up my exhausted horse. The mice pant and high five. The butler pretends not to recognize me. He shows me to the bedroom that used to be mine, and after all these years, I discover that little has changed. No matter what else the prince has done in here, the room reeks of sour virginity. The terror of that first night, the nauseating flashbacks, the glory of triumph quickly ceding to a tidal wave of guilt. My recurring nightmare was that my feet grew and grew.

The bedroom door opens, but instead of the prince, it's the Grand Duke. He holds a shoebox under his arm, puts a finger to his lips. Kneels before me and opens the box.

I half-expect they won't still fit. But they do.

And why? That's what I want to know: why is the most dubious part of my wardrobe the one that remains? Why this reinforcement of the illusion? Isn't it hard enough to stave off nihilism without the reminder that your youth was *completely implausible*? It couldn't have happened that way. It must've been a fever dream, a side effect, a hallucination.

But no, the glass slippers say. It happened. It was real. You were there. You were my family. And then you weren't.

"It's okay to be angry," the Grand Duke says. "It's okay to feel a lot of things."

I put the slippers back in the box, which the Duke slides under the bed. He kisses my cheek and shuts the door behind him.

The next time the door opens, it's the prince. "That creature outside," he says. "Belongs to you?"

"My trusty steed," I say. "Rides like a dream."

"You look familiar." He's wearing red silk pajama pants and a gold chain. He's trying to look cooler than he is, just like I'm trying to look sexier than I am. Somehow, it seems more real between us than it ever has before.

"People tell me that a lot," I say. I grab one of the posts on the bed like a pole and begin to dance.

YOU'RE NOT GOING TO DIE

Franny fought the gridlock on I-Drive for an hour only to arrive at the Palmscape Funerarium too late -- seven-thirty, the viewing had ended at seven. Instead of a funeral party she found a man in a reindeer suit. He slumped on the steps of the entrance to the building like some kind of misfit archangel, his fur matted and antlers askew. She put the car in park and closed her eyes. What else was there to do? On the seat beside her lay her duffle bag, the collection of t-shirts and underwear that reminded her of Marv, her marriage certificate pressed into a dictionary, the only book she owned. She'd kept the certificate safe between definitions for inadequate and incapable for three years, ever since she'd walked out on Marv in the middle of a *Jeffersons* rerun. She'd planned to dump the whole bag in the coffin. But even with her eyes closed, she could feel the Funerarium looming over her, white and sober and locked-down for the night.

When she opened her eyes, the man in the reindeer suit was prancing toward her, motioning with one paw for her to roll down the window, which she did. "You here for Marv?" he said through one of the eyes.

Franny nodded, and he handed her a flier. "After-life party," he said. "Two blocks north. Free food, free booze. Free rides in honor of Marv."

Centered on the flier was a picture of one of those roadside carnival rides that would-be entrepreneurs were forever setting up on I-Drive, siphoning the theme park crowds for a few months of profit before somebody got maimed or a mechanical glitch shut it down. The Avenger! it said at the top.

"What is this?" Franny said.

"It's The Avenger!" the reindeer suit said.

"Marv's?"

The suit nodded. "And Zimmy's."

Franny didn't know who Zimmy was. The name sounded like the wrong end of a cheerleader. She stood to leave, figuring she'd know The Avenger! when she saw it. "Hey," she said, indicating the suit's costume. "What's with this?"

He paused to take in her black, funereal jacket, her shiny shoes. "Theme funeral," he said and walked back up the steps to the Funerarium's entrance.

#

International Drive, with its t-shirt shops and family-style restaurants and proximity to at least three different theme parks, was sleazier than it first appeared. It was always crowded, and tonight the sidewalks were jammed from Wet 'N' Wild to Ripley's Believe It Or Not, a solid stretch of drunk tourists and sunburnt children and girls in thong bikinis. One parking lot hosted an impromptu wet t-shirt contest, and another offered discount Disney tickets. Flatbed trucks and jeeps loaded with bare-chested boys in Billabong shorts rolled along at five miles an hour, catcalling to girls. Franny, who'd opted to walk from the Funerarium, elbowed her way through the sunscreen-slick mass of them, the air around her loose and full as a cosmic water balloon. She passed a water park all under lights, bodies plunging over the edge of a six-story slide, pitching heads going round and round the drilling of the wave pool. When the waves ceased, the heads continued splashing, dragging each other below the surface.

The Avenger! appeared shortly: a cage, a couple of cranes on either side, and a mess of bungee cords. The name in poorly affixed neon. A fenced-off area of packed dirt surrounded it, a couple of bouncers – were they bouncers? – at the gate. Franny remembered the kid who'd gotten thrown off The Jackrabbit and landed on the highway, how after he'd died a small group of citizen activists had collected signatures to ban the rides. The law didn't pass. So here was The Avenger!, strung up and down with Christmas lights, people in costumes milling around the gate. Franny smiled. If she'd thought about it for a minute, she could've predicted that Marv would have a theme funeral. It was sweet and stupid, exactly what he would've wanted, if he'd had a chance to plan. A ceremony for people who believed anything could be solved by a costume change. Typical Marv, to be buried in drag. Typical Floridians, to pretend they were someplace they were not. She saw a stuffed water drop holding a beer, a guy in swim trunks wearing a witch's hat. A girl wearing a bikini under a fur coat. Everyone wore plastic leis, some had sombreros, and at least one person was in a headdress. She saw a bandana or two tied around the neck. A guy in a chef's hat was handing out corn dogs and Budweiser from the back of his truck. "What's the theme?" she asked one of the bouncers.

He handed her a purple lei. "You should come in, if you want to. We're almost full."

Franny hesitated. She was caught in one of those real life sci-fi moments, like this was a Hotel California of sorts, and if she went inside she'd never be able to get back out. Marv was swimming in the air around her, and who knew what kind of crazy shit ghosts could do, erasing your life and whatnot. She imagined that back at the Funerarium, the reindeer suit was hot-wiring her car and preparing to take over her life. It would motor down to the Egg Platter, a drive-thru breakfast place where she worked as a short order cook, and then come home to her current girlfriend, Denise, who would only balk for a minute over accepting Franny's replacement. The suit would nudge Franny out of reality just like the call from Marv's sister – *an accident, DOA, viewing Friday 5-7* – had sent Franny back into a state of imbalance she'd worked a good six months to get out of.

One phone call, and Franny was a wife again.

Except she wasn't.

Less than twenty-four hours ago, she'd been waking up in Denise's bed, her head in one corner and her feet in another. Denise had returned late, drunk and still pissed that Franny was *married?* and *to a man?* and *never thought to mention this?* She'd locked herself in the bathroom, and a few hours later Franny pried open the door with a screwdriver and found Denise passed out under the toilet, one arm stuck in an overturned trashcan. She didn't rally even when Franny turned on the faucet in the tub and sank into water that floated with debris from Denise's last shower. Franny hadn't washed. She'd listened to Denise breathe. Then she packed the duffle bag, sure that the next time she saw Denise, she'd be a woman without a past. Or, at least, the kind of woman whose past surrendered peacefully to the reality of the present.

But Franny's past was a breed all its own, a fighting variety, and when the bouncer handed her the lei, it seemed like she could hear Marv's cackling in the rustle of the plastic.

She gazed up at The Avenger!, saw two girls in grass skirts climb onto the platform, giggling into each other's hair. They entered a metal cage and sat on a hot, padded seat. An attendant wearing a stuffed shark head secured them inside with a padlock. The cage slingshot into the air on the bungee cords, rotated, and bounced back into position. The girls inside screamed.

He had some kind of business down there, the sister had said. *Doesn't that mean, legally, half's yours?*

And okay, yes, she could make that argument – legally – but Franny hadn't come out of greed. She hadn't come out of obligation, either. She was only still married to Marv because the divorce papers came back with signatures like "Miss me yet?" and "Try again." In fact, since she wasn't sure anymore why she *had* come, she thought she should probably just leave.

"You coming in?" the bouncer said.

"I guess," Franny said.

Beside her, the roar of traffic sounded unmistakably like applause.

#

Inside, she tried not to stare at the grass skirts swishing around the girls' thighs as they exited the ride, Marv's mourners all busty and nailpolished except her. Someone directed her to the Tiki bar, where a bare-chested man poured cocktails into plastic coconuts. She ordered a Mai Tai and tucked the umbrella behind her ear, then weaved through the crowd, pausing over a table set up to showcase Marv's life. Pictures, Franny realized with a start, that she'd taken herself. There was Marv at Gatorland just before they'd gotten kicked out; Marv toasting himself on his birthday after the rest of their party had left; Marv as a motorcycle tough, legs astride the bike that would later strand them both at a bar in Bithlo. There were no pictures of Franny, just Marv grinning at her, still somehow putting up his side of the argument. *Divorce this,* he said. *Just try and get rid of me.*

She circled the picture table once. Twice. And on her third lap was intercepted by a woman wearing a pair of yellow-lens sunglasses who stepped in front of Franny and said, "Stop." She was in her early forties, heavy enough that her own grass skirt didn't fit all the way around her waist, so she'd fixed it to her front with clear packing tape.

"I recognize you from the pictures," she said. "I cut you out." Her voice was broken with age and sadness and heavy smoking. She looked like a certain kind of woman Franny was used to seeing in backwoods gay bars – the kind who wanted to throw beer in your face and lick it off.

Ha, Franny thought. *Ha ha*. All these gorgeous women, and leave it to Marv to make the same mistake twice.

"You're smaller than I thought," the woman said. "I didn't think you'd show."

"I'm just here to say goodbye," Franny said loudly. For the record. She didn't know how many people recognized her. She'd refused to meet Marv's family even after she married him.

The woman stuck out a hand. "Don't suppose you know me," she said. "Name's Zimmy. It was my car he was driving." Zimmy held the handshake a beat too long, then dropped it abruptly. "Not a bad way to go, considering. Ball of flame and all that."

"Sorry about your car," Franny said.

Zimmy swept a wilted daisy from behind her ear and fingered it, pulling the petals out one by one and dropping them to the floor. "We had a thing," she said. "We weren't married – " she glared at Franny – "but it was serious. I mean, you didn't know him like I did." She sort of pounded her chest. "We were real, me and him."

"I don't doubt it," Franny said. "He ever hit you?"

Zimmy dropped the last petal. "Go back where you came from. Leave us alone." She walked over to the crane that composed the largest part of The Avenger! and put her hands against it like she was going to push it over. Someone rubbed her back. Franny stared at the final flower petal, which had fluttered underneath the photograph table and was curled up at one end, like a smirk.

He loved me not. Franny had been counting.

#

She drank her second Mai Tai at the bar and took her third to a group of mourners nearby: a trio of Mickey ears and two women in cat suits. She sidled up between the women and said, "Hey."

"Hey," they said.

"So how did you all know Marv?" Franny asked, clutching her sticky cup.

The three people in Mickey ears dropped their eyes, and one of the cat suits whispered, "They're from Ohio. They didn't know this was a funeral."

Franny grinned. Marv, she thought, would've loved that. She remembered what it'd been like to be new here, to be young and tan all the time, Marv standing naked on the hotel bed saying, "Let's get married" in the same tone as he'd said, the night before, "Let's get trashed." Franny had agreed to both, thinking she could do worse. Marv was a stand-up sort of guy, not one you had to worry about getting shot or OD-ing. He sometimes wrote bad checks, sometimes got too frisky at the titty bar, but most of the time he was just a guy, working and chasing tail, decent in every other way. Didn't have a lot of illegitimate babies, didn't steal from old folks or deal to kids. Your average fuck-up.

He'd been Franny's ticket to a world where her currency was no good. Marv didn't care that she'd grown up in a trailer in a Podunk town outside Jacksonville, and he didn't even ask about her stepfather, or her experience with child services. These were the too-common details in the lives of Girls Like Her, repeated so often that they either explained too much or ceased to explain anything at all. He assumed certain givens about her life, and Franny was relieved not to have to clarify. "Let's get married," he'd said, and Franny had thought, *I'll take it.*

After the ceremony, she'd given Marv a blowjob in the back of their rented Mustang, and then they'd ordered celebratory double cheeseburgers at the drive-thru. The blowjob had been lackluster; the hamburger, delicious. They'd been so happy that they decided not to go home. It was as simple as that. Franny got a job at The Egg Platter and Marv at the Alpine Slide, and they found a cheap apartment furnished with a battered pullout couch, and they made it work. It'd been perfect the first year, Franny's ideal arrangement, until one night Marv backhanded her in bed, drunk, and then said, "Do that to me now." And, when she refused, "Not even if I want you to?"

So she'd done it. And enjoyed it.

At first, it was like a crime she was getting away with. A way to exercise some of the rage she found hidden just below the surface. The first night, she'd hit him hard. Thinking she'd shut him up. Angry, and somewhat embarrassed, at what he'd done. She'd been hit before. She'd hit back before. But it'd never been anything near foreplay. She expected to feel guilty afterwards. But she'd found that living in Orlando involved a gradual leeching of the real world, a tacit acceptance of fairy tale. The next day Marv acted like nothing had happened. And Franny found herself not only able, but willing to believe that nothing had. She had not tapped into something dangerous in herself. She was not, at heart, a dangerous person.

If he'd have stopped there, they might've stayed together longer. But Marv wanted to see Franny lose control.

"I don't think that's a good idea," she said.

"Don't think about it," Marv said. He put her hands on his body, and though the touch began gentle, she could feel the desire like a kind of arthritis. Her hands wanted to ball. To squeeze. It was work to keep them open. She'd never felt like this before. She didn't want to feel it now.

"I'm afraid I'll kill you," she whispered. He didn't think she could. But sometimes when he was sleeping a certain way, or even just tilting his head to the side, she could see a vein fluttering in his neck. She wished she didn't notice things like that, the places where people were weak. She watched the vein. He didn't know she did that.

"You won't," he said. "I trust you."

She moved her hands to his neck, touched that spot where the vein sometimes was. She couldn't see it when he was standing.

"So you're not going to die," she said. She circled his neck. "Then what's the thrill?"

He lifted his chin. Closed his eyes. "Darlin', I've got thrills," he said.

"I don't know if I like you like this." She took her hands away.

He put them back. "I like you like this," he said.

But he didn't understand. She didn't want her love to be tied up in violence. The two couldn't coexist in her. One tried to take over, and the violence always won. She knew she couldn't be trusted. She knew she'd take it too far.

And she did. It just didn't happen the way she thought. It was how far he let her go that was the problem. After two close calls, she tried to cut Marv off. When he refused, she went looking elsewhere. What she found was women. Safe women, gentle women, women who were so soft it was impossible to want to hurt them. She finally left Marv, but he didn't so much as flinch.

"You'll be back," he said calmly, not lifting his eyes from the TV screen. "I know you ain't no goddamn dyke."

#

It wasn't until after Franny had downed her fourth Mai Tai, tapping glasses with the trio from Ohio, that Zimmy announced she was going to ride The Avenger! Franny had watched her saunter around the grounds, punching people in the arm, licking the corner of her mouth when she looked up at The Avenger! All swagger and heft. She looked like she wouldn't mind losing control; she looked like she'd never had it to begin with. "You all know," Zimmy said to the crowd, "that Marv and I had just upgraded a new feature to the ride when he died. It's never been tested. Until now." She hesitated, and the attendant said, "You sure, Zim?" Franny snickered.

"She's scared to ride her own ride," she said to no one. "That's hilarious."

"Jesus," Zimmy said, following the sound to Franny's face. "You are something else." She walked toward Franny slowly, everybody watching. The yellow lenses turned her eyes green. Her gaze nearly emitted heat. She looked like she might really hit Franny, but one of the cat suits stepped forward to lead her away. "I told you," Zimmy said to Franny. "Go home."

"Hey." Franny held her fifth Mai Tai in the air and hugged her duffel bag under her arm. She looked up at Zimmy in a way that tried to be friendly. "Come on, girl. Let's do this together."

Zimmy shook her head.

"Ride The Avenger with me," Franny said, "and I'll leave." She looked at the bouncers, who looked at Zimmy.

The attendant in the shark's head secured the cage to the launch and opened the door for them, and Zimmy whispered something to him. Franny fell into the cage. Sat on the bench seat beside Zimmy, who handed her a pilled seatbelt to fasten across both of their hips. The cranes on either side of them were strung with bare bulbs; the bungee cords appeared worn. "You don't look scared," Zimmy said.

"You don't look straight," Franny blurted. She dropped her head.

They sat in silence for several moments. Franny glanced over to see Zimmy squeeze her eyes shut. "Okay, Marv," she said. "Here we are."

She actually patted Franny's leg, as if to comfort her. As if to say, *I know you loved him, too.* Franny's stomach burbled. The man in the reindeer suit was in the crowd now, and she wondered if she could sneak into the Funerarium, slip the duffel bag into Marv's coffin without anyone noticing. One of the t-shirts in her bag was from the Alpine Slide, and it said, I Went Alpine Sliding in Florida. There'd been ice skating, too, on a synthetic rink. Franny smoothed her pant legs, and Zimmy yelled, "Can we do this?" and the attendant pulled a lever.

One minute Franny was watching the stuffed water drop flick her off, and the next her head was glued to the back of the cage. The pressure on her chest was heavy as a body, too heavy to yell the way Zimmy was hollering Marv's name, the way Franny had yelled it after their first close call. He'd tried to explain it to her afterward, what it felt like, but she'd been too freaked out to hear him. *Your face*, she kept saying, shaking her head like she could loosen the image. *You turned blue.*

It took a long time for The Avenger! to reach its apex, and Franny half-expected the bungee cords to snap, the cage to fly into space. But the cords caught, faithfully, and the cage held a sickening beat mid-air, pitching Franny and Zimmy toward the ground. The contents of Franny's stomach flowed into her esophagus, and her head swung forward. Below her the city spread out, sparkling in a way that broke Franny's heart. She closed her eyes for the plummet, but instead there was a mechanical whizzing sound from the cranes, and the bungees snapped taut. The cage bobbled uncertainly.

"That's my boy!" Zimmy shouted, stomping happily. She leaned down and held a thumb's up to the crowd below, who responded with a spattering of applause. "New feature," she said to Franny. "Freeze frame." She looked over. "You okay?"

Franny rubbed her eyes. "How long do we sit here?"

"Don't know," Zimmy said. "That's the beauty of it."

Franny looked out over the city again. "It all looks so nice from up here," she said.

Zimmy gazed outward, too. "It's a nice place."

"You think so?" Franny said. "Really?"

"I don't know," Zimmy said. "Marv loved it."

"And you loved Marv."

Zimmy was quiet, and then she spoke. "Tell me why you really came here."

"Respect?" Franny said. "Closure?"

Zimmy shook her head. "Something else."

There was so much else Franny wanted that she got choked up trying to answer. Zimmy rolled her eyes. "You're a piece of work," she said. She slid an arm around Franny, python-like. "I know all about you. You really fucked him up."

She bent at the elbow. A head-lock. "This what you like to do?"

Franny went limp. *Oh, Marv,* she thought. He was everywhere, in the wet air around her, in the hinges of the metal cage. Sitting like a puppeteer above her, all sorrow and punishment. She could smell his stale scent in Zimmy's clothes, his Marlboro's on her breath. *Half of what was his,* the sister had said. "Oh, Marv," she whispered. She unbuckled the seatbelt.

"What the hell," Zimmy said. "You're going to kill us." She waved one arm to the attendant below in some kind of signal, released Franny's neck. Franny stood. Turned so she was facing Zimmy. Zimmy looked into her eyes and said, "Do it."

"I'm not going to hit you," Franny said. "I just wondered if you would." She stopped. "This sounds crazy, but would you," and she straddled Zimmy and kissed her full on the mouth. She forced her tongue into Zimmy's mouth. Felt Zimmy's tongue jerk to attention before Zimmy remembered herself and bit down.

"No," Zimmy said, sadly but not convincingly.

"This what you like to do?" Franny said. She kissed Zimmy again and waited for the bite. She grabbed handfuls of shirt and skin, thinking, *Marv, Marv, what have you done to me?* Thinking of the second close-call, her hands around Marv's neck, when his body had locked into a kind of spasm, and Franny had been fascinated, watching him drain away. The change in him had been immediate. He'd been so vulnerable, so dependent. She'd fallen in love with him for the first time.

Then he'd come back to life.

Zimmy succeeded in freeing one of her hands, wound the seatbelt around herself and the back of Franny's legs – and then they plunged. Franny clung to the grating and Zimmy's body, but her face smacked the top of Zimmy's head when they reached bottom, and her nose began to bleed. After the first drop, the cage bounced maniacally, knocking Franny around. Finally it clanked down, and the attendant opened the door.

"You're insane," Zimmy said.

"Holy shit," the attendant said. "What happened?"

Zimmy stumbled onto the platform and kept walking. Franny grabbed her duffel bag and said, "Nothing, I'm fine, it's okay," and rushed over to the Port-a-Potty, where she thought she might get sick but didn't, so hovered over the seat trying to piss. She took out the dictionary and shook it over the floor. The marriage certificate fell out, and Franny dangled it over the hole between two fingers. Then she put it back in the book and put the book back in her bag. The certificate was, she thought, the only evidence that she'd ever loved someone. That she'd once been capable of love.

She threw her bloody shirt down the toilet instead and dug through her bag to find a replacement. She found one Marv had bought her as a joke, before the joke became truth. A pink shirt with the word "Dyke" written in sparkly letters. No one else would understand the sick humor of the shirt, how Marv had understood and not understood her. Not even Denise. She put it on. Heard murmuring behind her, the way people talked to their dates in movie theaters.

Something fell hard against the Port-a-Potty. She zipped up and went around back. The reindeer suit was there with the attendant, the guy in the shark head, standing over the girl in the fur coat, who was now topless underneath. She smiled at Franny, her eyelids low, slouched against the toilet. She'd either fallen or been thrown. She couldn't seem to get Franny into focus, and her head was limp on her neck. She looked vaguely familiar, somebody Franny would've known back when she and Marv were together. She raised a shaky hand, pointed at Franny.

"Want to join?" she said and tried to laugh but, failing that, slid further inside her coat.

"Shut the fuck up," the reindeer suit said. The other guy took off his shark head and threw it on the ground. They both walked off.

"Assholes," the girl slurred.

Franny nodded. She looked at the shark head, its open mouth biting the ground. She picked it up. Put it on. It smelled like beer and sweat inside, and she had trouble breathing. The girl beside her clapped weakly.

Franny found the eyeholes and in a few minutes, she'd grown accustomed to the tunnel vision and could move easily. The Avenger! shot into the air, catapulting Marv's survivors into the wet night. Franny heard it, but her eyes were fixed on the girl: her loose boobs, her teeth. "Want to ride with me?" Franny said. She moved closer, her hands finding the way.

ORIGIN STORY

Once a girl found a stray tornado. She lured it inside with a dog biscuit. It was a juvenile, so she kept it in a box beside her bed. Sort of brindle, like her second dog. But blurrier. Twice a day, she fed it dry leaves in a stainless bowl. It preferred saltwater to fresh. She named it Tor because she was not particularly creative and liked to call things what they were.

Training left her bruised. The tornado pulled on the leash, gagged over the collar. Once it bit her, and she had to get six stitches in her palm. The Urgent Care doctor made a joke about fashioning her a new lifeline.

"A prosthetic future," he called it.

"My life will be different now," she told him, thinking of the tornado. "That's for sure."

When asked about the origin of the wound, she blamed it on a vicious, unidentifiable dog, then regretted her choice when the doctor brought up rabies. She didn't know if tornadoes could carry rabies or not, and it wasn't the kind of thing she could easily find out. She didn't know anyone else to whom this had happened, and internet searches proved useless, so she went ahead and got the shots.

At home, the tornado sniffed the raw gridwork of her hand and spun placidly on the floor all night, as sorry-seeming as a tornado could be.

#

In two weeks, it reached shoulder height; in a month, it outgrew her. She wasn't sure if she should keep it, but she didn't like goodbyes. The tornado filled the house in a way that seemed familiar, all clamor and bustle. Anything not secured blew around wildly, so she boxed up most of her things. The wind made the faucet spray her right in the face if she forgot to shut the bathroom door. The windows rattled; her hair tangled. When the tornado got excited, the ceiling fans spun in reverse. When she spoke gibberish into its funnel, the words came back in order.

Everything happens for a reason, it said.

Take all the time you need, it said.

Don't flip out on me, Susan, it said.

She didn't know who Susan was, but of course the house was haunted. Anyone could've told her that. It'd been fully furnished when she moved in. She'd brought a few clothes and books, hung and stacked them next to the existing ones, and now she couldn't remember which were legitimately hers. The handwriting in the books was so similar, and the clothes fit so well, that they might as well have been her own.

The yards in this part of town were built to prevent neighborliness, with aggressive layers of hedges and fences and underbrush, so no one need know the new pet/roommate she'd acquired. She had one neighbor who she saw exactly twice a year, when he asked permission to collect blackberries from her yard in the summer and when he reminded her to top her trees in the fall, which she never did. He lived with a wife the girl had not met or even seen. She only knew the wife existed because her neighbor referred to himself in the plural, the way married couples do. For all she knew, when he said 'we,' he could've meant himself and his tornado.

"We were wondering if you're going to use all those blackberries," he'd said this past spring, as he did every year.

"Help yourself," the girl said, as she always did. "We won't be using them."

When he came by in the fall, she hadn't answered the door. Her neighbor must've heard the breaking glass, the pounding and yelling, and assumed what he assumed. He didn't return.

#

Her second dog ran away, so she taught the tornado to fetch. It was easy to teach when it wanted to learn, which made her suspect it was older than she'd initially thought. Maybe tornadoes didn't have ages, or maybe, for them, size wasn't proportionate to age. It seemed to grow and shrink with its moods, if you could call them moods, though not in any predictable way. Its happiness posed as much of a danger as its anger, the way both generated mid-sized ball lightning that left scorch marks on the wood floors and burned holes in the walls. She cleaned up or repaired its messes, and coached the tornado to contain itself as best it could. Her favorite times were when, in sleep, its wall clouds relaxed and covered the room in soft, gray fog. Some nights the girl climbed inside the funnel and slept suspended two feet off the ground in a white-noise wind-hive where she could not hear her dreams.

Other nights, she dreamt that the trees she'd neglected to top as advised fell and crushed her in her sleep.

To teach it how to fetch, she had to take the tornado outside. They started in the back yard. Once she threw a stick, and the tornado brought back an apple tree. She quickly harvested the carefully-tended fruit and shoved the tree husk into a ditch where the previous occupants had discarded their Christmas trees. She'd stumbled on the Christmas tree graveyard while searching for a suitable graveyard-graveyard for her first dog, who'd died right after she'd moved in. At the time, she thought the dog must've gotten into something poisonous in the overgrown yard – mushrooms, perhaps, or bella donna – but after a thorough search, she'd found nothing. She buried him by the woodshed, nervous over every shovelful. The house was haunted, after all; who knew what she might dig up? She found nothing but rocks, so many big rocks that it took her all day to dig deep enough, which was okay because she wasn't looking forward to the next step, which was dragging the dog into it. She didn't call anyone because, in that part of town, there was no one to call. She'd gone over to her neighbor's house, but no one was home.

The largest rock, she'd used as a headstone. The rest she piled into a decorative fire pit. She didn't intend to ever build a fire.

She tried again. She threw the ball, and the tornado brought back a tire.

She threw the ball, and the tornado brought back a cracked windshield.

She threw the ball, and the tornado brought back the rest of the wrecked car, which she pushed into the street in front of her neighbor's house.

She didn't like where this was headed, so she tried throwing a stuffed toy instead. The tornado brought back her second dog.

She buried him by the woodshed with the first. The tornado spun the hole in five minutes flat. It seemed a little too happy to help. This was how the girl came to understand that the tornado needed to go. She suspected that living with a tornado would mean having to regularly bury things, and she wanted to be done with burying things now.

She put its bowl outside and shut the door. What was she supposed to do? There wasn't a shelter she could call, and she certainly wasn't turning it over to a meteorologist or a storm chaser. It was a stout and ferocious tornado, but also, in its way, a little naïve about the outside world. A little sheltered. Stuck outside, it pawed at the door with mid-level winds, whirled in a slumped way. The girl tried to feel good about being able to brush her hair for the first time in months, to read a book. But even with her bedroom door closed, she could hear its sad scraping out front. Her bed felt muggy and stagnant, her body feverish. She'd become accustomed to the noise of the wind, and now understood what people meant when they called silence deafening.

The tornado stayed on the stoop the whole first night. In the morning, she filled its bowl and sat in the yard, throwing balls that it brought back exactly as they were, as if obedience was the solution.

After a while, she went back inside. She left the tornado out, and again, it stayed on the stoop all night.

The third night, it left. She listened to it go, holding her breath. It was back by morning, sleeping heavily, its wall clouds wispy and discolored.

The fourth night, it didn't come back.

The girl tried to read but couldn't concentrate. She walked around her neighborhood, telling herself she wasn't listening for the tornado, looking into the dark windows of the houses around her. The wrecked car was where she'd left it. The trees tossed ominously overhead.

She considered leaving town but didn't like to drive. Anyway, there was nowhere else to go. She could always change her mind, she thought, leave another night, or come back, or do something altogether different. It was important to remember, during hard times, that you could always do something altogether different.

When she got home, she turned on the TV, something she hadn't done in all the time she'd lived here. The first station was network news, so she watched that. She watched it night after night while waiting to see if the tornado would return. People went missing during this time because people were always going missing one way or another, so the girl didn't think anything of the reports she saw. Except for one. The one was her own. The reporters seemed to have confused her with someone else. It was her face on the screen, but they called her a wife and mother. They showed a picture of her street with the wrecked car in front of her neighbor's house. The car must've belonged to the missing woman, she thought, which sort of explained the confusion. And sort of did not. Then a cop with streaming blue eyes said her name into the camera. His pronunciation was a little off, but it was definitely her name. He looked like a fountain, like not really crying. It would be unusual for a cop to cry like that. The tears disappeared under his chin.

The girl went to the police department with a case of mistaken identity.

"That poor woman deserves to be found, whoever she is," she told the front desk. "She has a husband and children."

She was given a can of soda and told to wait right there.

She waited for a long time, long enough for the soda to give her a stomachache and then for the stomachache to subside. Long enough to wonder if she should leave, to give it five more minutes, and to think at the end of the five minutes, *What if I leave and they come right now?* Long enough to wonder what if she really did have a husband and children that she'd somehow managed to forget, and was that even possible, and if it was, how, and did it even matter if it was possible or not if it happened to you, and hasn't the whole idea of impossibility gone stale in this world of medical miracles and technological marvels, and isn't the real impossibility life itself, like how does anyone survive infancy let alone childhood with so many dangers stacked against them, a list of dangers so long you could start now and never reach the end? Long enough to wonder how much of one's future could be sewn into the skin by a qualified doctor.

Eventually, a uniformed officer emerged from behind a partition and lumbered toward her. His body puffed out, like it wanted to burst from its clothes. At first she thought he must be a superhero. A breeze blew back her bangs as he approached. Her ears popped. He moved his jaw like it was a new appendage, then said her name with the same incorrect pronunciation, but also like a question.

"Do I know you?" she said.

"You must," he said.

She rose, cupped her hands around her mouth, and blew speech sounds into his ear.

"Time heals all wounds," he said.

She understood, and was both afraid and intrigued. She was a mixed-up mess of many things, which was why people always trusted her.

They walked to a private room, him leaning heavily on her arm, nearly pulling her down. His skin vibrated, vented from every pore. She figured he couldn't be too dangerous in a public place, which was the logic for strangers, but not storms. He was both and neither. As so often happened to her, she had no idea how to protect herself. She was charmed by the lengths he'd gone to for her, and she wanted to believe that a man was somehow safer than a tornado.

This is called magical thinking.

"What should I call you?" she asked him.

"Whatever you want to," he said.

She called him Tor. He gave her bold coffee which made her rattle on about her life, all the things he didn't know, which was mostly a catalog of news stories. She thought of the tornado as *he* now because of the human form. He kept forgetting to blink, then scrubbing with fists at his eyes when they blurred over. She realized that a body must be a lot to keep track of.

Finally he shoved back his chair, stood, and said abruptly, "Maybe I could visit you sometime."

She put down her cup. "Yes. Yes, I think so."

"Maybe that time is right now."

"Oh," she said. "Okay."

Sometimes the girl did things without questioning why she was doing them, even though she knew the thing she was doing was exactly the kind of thing she should question. This was one of those times.

As she led him down the hall, down the elevator, and out into the day, she thought instead about how many of the people they passed might be inhabited by storms. It would explain a lot, she thought. It might even provide some comfort, letting humanity off the hook as it did.

On the train home, she thought it again. Suddenly people seemed so much more understandable to her.

The cop was not just any storm; she hadn't forgotten that he'd killed her dog. But it was kind of like when your cat brought home a dead bunny. You could keep the cat inside or get rid of the cat, but you didn't get mad at it for being a cat.

So she took the tornado into her home again, this time as a cop in a uniform he wouldn't take off. He sat unevenly on a stool at her counter, working at good posture and polite behavior, and attempted to drink a glass of water by pouring it in his mouth and jerking his head back. When she told him to make himself at home, he collapsed on the floor. She lay beside him for a while, unsure what was possible or appropriate.

"I missed you," she said.

He took her hand, but while she waited for what would come next, he began to snore. The snoring sounded like a waterfall and smelled like cut grass. When it was clear he was not going to wake anytime soon, she turned on the TV news, but someone else had gone missing, a man, so she quickly changed the station. Landed on a show called *How Are We All Not Dead?* that investigated the lethal potential embedded in everyday objects as evidenced in actual police and autopsy reports, narrated intermittently by a cartoon pirate. Number 42: stapler. Number 43: vacuum. The show was too aware of its attempts to be funny to be funny. It couldn't figure out its genre. The girl had too much time to think about it while the cop's snores spun in eddies around the room.

At some point she slept, trying not to sleep. She didn't want him to wake without her. She dreamt she was a wife and mother, but her husband was a tornado and her children were dogs.

She woke feeling grateful, and, almost without thinking, laid her body on top of the cop's. He stirred, the tornado already pacing inside, the human skin like a gate from which it longed to burst. "Are you able to come out?" she whispered in his ear.

"If you want me to," he whispered back.

She didn't. She blew gibberish into the cop's ear and he said, "We need to talk" and "It's nobody's fault" and "Don't leave like this, Susan."

"Who is Susan?" she said, and he said, "I thought you knew."

The tornado pressed on her through the cop's body, and she pressed back in a familiar way. She still didn't know what was appropriate, but now she knew what was possible. They both unzipped but stayed mostly clothed. The tornado didn't know what it was doing, but the girl did. During, she thought they might be in love. After, she thought not.

"You can't stay in there forever," she told him, but she was also fishing for information.

"No," he said. "But if I could?"

She felt terrible. Her heart kept jumping out of windows before she could talk it down.

"I can't stay here either," she told him. "This house is extremely haunted."

"I never noticed," he said.

She left barefoot. The trees were swaying as they always were. Someone, maybe her neighbor, had pushed the wrecked car further down the street. The houses were all unlit, though she could see those peripheral movements that disappeared when you looked at them directly.

Once again, something was happening to her that she could not explain or even tell anyone about. But everyone walked around with impossible things lodged in them like splinters. They had survived what they could not have survived. They had lost what they could not bear to lose.

THE MORAL

The youngest daughters grow up to be judges, sentence their stepmothers to rehab. Princes donate the wolves to prison puppy programs. Mothers no longer worry about starvation; they worry about excess sugar. They live in gingerbread houses with underwater mortgages, clip coupons for buy-one-get-one boneless whatever. They file chapter thirteen with witches who are lawyers – more overtaxed than wicked. When they need to dispose of their children, they don't send them to the woods. They leave them in the car, the pool, the Walmart. They tell their children not to tell. Their children bounce satellite signals off the stars.

#

Once a fortune teller in a souvenir shop pierced my navel. I was thirteen in cutoffs; no one else would do it. She said I'd get infected. I met you twenty years and ten failed inseminations later: handshake, swipe, receipt. You looked like a fortune and promised results. Basement office with baby pictures on the ceiling. You in your white coat, buxom between my legs; my wife at my head, resurrecting a vial of frozen sperm in her fist. You examined the sperm under a microscope, offered us a better vial from a stash in your freezer. Looked at me like I had no wife. Blood in a needle, light in my eyes. Close as a kiss with alcohol on your breath. You ran a hand over my torso and a tube into my uterus, gave the guarantee real doctors never give. I flinched and thought, *Don't flinch.*

That night, the belly piercing, long since closed, erupted stretch marks. *No need to pee on a stick,* I told my wife. *Whatever she gave us, it worked.*

The stretch marks matched your scars exactly.

#

The mother pushed her kid through a window or didn't secure the screen.

The mother rolled on her baby, unbuckled in a hot car she was driving off the bridge to sell them into sex work.

She was drunk/high/packing heat and prescription weight loss pills. She gave the kids three wishes. The minivan floated into the sunset.

#

I have a crush, I told my wife. A flutter, a flinch, a thought where the thought was not supposed to be. A grammatical error, an equation: where X was an utterance, then Y was a corresponding flush. I booked elective appointments, flirted in stirrups half-dressed on white paper. When you called me honey, the word acquired density and its own orbit.

Blood flooded the surface. Where X was a reflex, then Y was a blush.

The babies on the ceiling disapproved. You didn't ask why my wife opted not to come. Your mouth was a tantrum, mine a lit fuse. *Here's a touch,* you said, but no warning next time. The atmosphere, strung with punctuation.

Shh without sound is a kiss. So hush. Where X was you, there was no Y.

#

The mother dropped the baby and left the gate unlatched.

She fled the scene and didn't call 911.

She failed to respond/account/appear/thrive.

She left the children alone in the crib, in a car seat under the kitchen table, wrapped in blankets near the stove, with the addict/boyfriend/grandmother while she went to the store for more pop.

#

No matter that I didn't know the father, or the other, or where the Y was from. What bloomed inside belonged to you. Your stash from the fridge. Infection, maybe, or a genetic tripwire tripped. Suddenly there was pleasure in everything: the sexuality of napkins. Cleavage in a chicken breast. At the Super Buffet, I ordered a fruity cocktail served in a fishbowl with two straws and drunk-dialed your number. *You knocked me up*, I said, *which means this guppy's yours.* You came with a car.

You came like confirmation. I mauled you in the lot, ringed finger twisting your belt loops. Illness, anomaly, Not My Normal. What is a fetus but an index, a guide to yours and mine? Alien, aquatic, gills and a tail. What bloomed inside was the animal way of desire. You came and changed the scenery. The air around you thick for wolfing.

#

The mother was off her meds/rocker/high horse, but it was a wardrobe malfunction and she didn't read the fine print. She set the baby down for a minute, and when she returned he was grown up and resentful, emancipated, suing her for loss of innocence. He had tattoos of itemized lists and search results, and she dreamed that she woke up from the dream but when she woke up her baby still wasn't there.

#

We met at the park where pregnant cats nested in the live oaks. You scattered shrimp tails and crab shells on the ground, laughed and said they'd eat anything. You were equal parts sex appeal and rage, and I wondered how you ever got a job. The cats thunked to the ground, branches retracting. They moved like they were caught in traps. You told me about your childhood in a way that made me ashamed, so I backed you against the tree and changed the subject. Your hands searched me for something like proof, and my body let slip the secret. I wanted your wanting. The cats somersaulted; the baby purred. You turned me around when I tried to look you in the eye. All of us licking scars we called wounds.

#

The mother won't return our calls and we are getting impatient/worried/litigious. We will fight for monogamy and custody. We'll ask her to remove her jewelry and anything in her pockets. She'll take off her nails and cleats, unscrew her teeth. Into the bin go oilcan and heart.

She should've never had children. She should've never grown up. We'll serve her with papers, banish her from the castle, lock her in the closet.

#

I left the cold night for your cold apartment. It looked like a crime scene that hadn't happened yet. I imagined my chalk outline in the kitchen, my body across the bed. My sprawled limbs would answer the detective's questions, my bones would form stories I hadn't known I was telling. A crime of passion, one way or the other. The line between defense and desire so hard to call.

Why, then, did I go in? Why did I stay? Because touch can be food, and what starving person won't cross police tape to eat? When you looked at me, everything levitated. The naked things adorned themselves. The bare things trimmed each other, the lonely things rushed to prepare. Your words grew fingers and spread.

You operated me faster than common sense. I got in the bath, and you climbed on top, scrubs still on. I sunk, and the baby floated between us. Your heart an anvil. Your breath planting flag after flag.

Later that night I called the cops on you. They stared at my belly and said I seemed like a nice lady.

No chalk. No sirens. No one twisted in sheets, reaching for the door.

#

She'll lose the case/game/last ten pounds. She'll see her children under supervision during visiting hours. She'll take parenting classes and get her degree. She'll work two jobs to support her kids/habit/ambition. If life gave her lemons, she'd eat lemons. But life never gives her lemons, so she buys them in bulk. Halves them, salts them, sucks out the juice.

#

When it was time, I kneeled at my wife's bedside with wet pants: *let's go.* She didn't ask where I'd been, or where my car was. She helped me to her car and drove. The obligatory traffic. The story so familiar I don't have to say how we almost didn't make it. Say instead that the car broke down and I birthed the baby on a gas station floor, the attendant a fat man named Slim. Say that it was summer, and the cicadas had heated themselves to sparking. That it was you strapping on a mask and cutting the cord.

That I was your wife, or that my wife was you.

Say that when it was my time, you were sober. That I woke in bed, not on the floor. That you hadn't hidden my keys so I wouldn't do what I did, which was to go home first. Wake my wife.

Say that when I woke on your apartment floor, still in my coat, I wanted to leave you far behind. Say that I didn't search your pockets, find my keys, leave them there.

Say that when it was my time, I didn't kiss you goodbye in your sleep.

#

The mother is all right, she's fine, she's great, and no she doesn't need a break and no she doesn't need a nap and no she doesn't want a sandwich or coffee or vitamins and no she doesn't want her prescription filled, sure she's a little keyed up but that's normal, given the situation, given the time of night and the amount of booze and the pepper spray she's taken to carrying in her coat pocket, right next to the car keys, given the feeling that wells up and says *fight* when there's no reason to fight, in the middle of the day while she's nursing the baby and watching TV – a whole series on reptile attacks alone – she just needs a run/a dollar/a minute to herself, she just needs to rest her eyes, she just needs the baby to stop screaming, and no she doesn't think of hurting herself, and no she doesn't think of hurting anyone else, and no she'd never hurt the baby, of course not, but did you know that some reptiles eat their young, and what is that like, to swallow what you've birthed, to take it back, to undo what seems so done?

#

My baby bore me into hunger. He came equipped with reflexes for rooting, sucking, tongue-thrust. I lacked instinct so they sent a lactation consultant. The feedings so painful they curled my toes, the colostrum's path of pins and needles. My nipples looked chewed and I swore I felt teeth, but the lactation consultant pried open the slick silver of the baby's mouth to show me his gums, unbroken. Nothing was as it seemed. She dipped the pacifier in wine she called water and handed me the hospital list of meats and desserts. Taught me to hold my baby like a football. Later I dreamed I woke covered in needles which the lactation consultant said were for infertility. I reminded her I'd just given birth, but she shushed me and whispered, *We need to change the ending.* The next time I woke I was pregnant again. Then a nurse wheeled in my baby, and then the nurse was you.

He has your mouth, I said.

#

The mother puts the keys in the ignition. Needle in her arm.

She doesn't go quietly.

She leaves the mess for someone else.

#

You came to the hospital with cake and daisies, talked APGAR scores with the nurse, made a display of professionalism. Slipped me my keys, no memory of why you had them. Survival depends upon forgetting. The residue pain of childbirth is nothing like the pain of childbirth, but it's all we have left to feel. The body turns toward forgiveness. You took my hand under the sheet. I accepted a slice of cake.

Or: the mouth isn't good at knowing what's good for it.

#

She left behind twin boys. A loving husband. No note.

Left chains of iron and dandelion. Chipped white plates. Rows of textbook remainders. A hive of startled bees.

The note would've said: there's a roast in the oven.

The twin boys were found in the woods, each clutching half a plate.

#

The neck straightens, the limbs flex. Still we swallow what we can't stomach. We say *bite your tongue.* We say *spit it out.* A conversation can be a dish served on fire. At home, I left my wife and baby for the blow-up bed in the spare room, then woke sweaty with a milk-soaked shirt at midnight, desperate to talk to you. Wanting to be more than calories. Fever tasted like pennies, engorgement like ink. I dialed the breastfeeding hotline, and the ringing tasted like tea. I told the hotline that I had a problem with clogged ducts and recklessness. That I had an unhealthy appetite for things I couldn't endure. *I'm trying to control myself,* I said, *but it's not working.* The hotline asked if I'd like to speak to a doctor. I heard the click, pictured the line being transferred to you.

Salt dough. Bergamot. Nectar.

#

The mother knew about the girls upstairs. She held the baby under. Left the family dog/rat/boa alone with the kids. Gave them sips/tokes/PINs. Left the handgun/car key where they could find it.

Refused the shot.

The Neighborhood

Did not properly install the car seat.

It was her responsibility to know the combination.

To know when to pull the plug/play dead/refuse the Koolaid.

#

The baby was a fertile land for contaminants. All milk-fat and mounded flesh, suckling yeast and heartbreak. I buttered skin, swabbed tooth bugs, combed cradle cap. I hiked my shirt on the way to your apartment, drove with my knees, filled zipper bags with blue-green milk. The plastic suck, the nipple's pathetic gasp. I do it so I won't squirt when I get to you. I do it so I'll have something to bring home after happy hour. I pump-n-dump so I don't have to think about trace elements or blood content. You keep dead clams in your fridge, bodies pulsed out like tongues. Your tin cans are swollen as lips.

Botulism has no taste, nor paralytic poisoning, nor infidelity. You kiss where the baby has bitten and tell me the broken skin tastes sweet.

#

Her children are obese. They curse and bite. They binge on fast food and can't read. Their teeth rot. Their blood sugar is off the charts. They're in the ground/branches/slammer. They live in motel rooms/gutted vans/hidden chambers. The police found three dozen cats in the home. Rust has eaten the pipes. The baby has a nasty diaper rash.

Mischief can be a group of rats; a wreck is just a collection of seabirds.

#

At some point, I understood that things were what we called them. You weren't *troubled*; you were a disaster. I wasn't *struggling*; I was fucked. I called honey *poison* until the baby turned one, then I called it *sweet*. I called my mother/sister/wife and told her off. I called foul, called bluff, called the question. I called in sick. I was not like or as a storm; I hurricaned. I thundered. I was shot through with electricity. It was my body that determined the temperature of the room, and honey, that room was on fire. At some point, I started calling things exactly what they were.

#

We say she's ill. Brainwashed. Unfit. We say we don't know how she could do it. We say, *What kind of a mother?* We say put her away. Good riddance. Better off without her. We say she seemed so nice. We say we didn't see it coming.

We say ding dong, the witch is dead.

We say she needs help. We say someone should help her. We say social services and bootstraps. We say failure of the medical/educational/penal system. We say let down your long hair, why won't you let down your long hair, what kind of a mother won't let down her long hair?

We say take a bump/drink/bite. We say they'll be fine. We say old enough. We say trust us. We say sign here. We say do what's best. We say trust your instinct.

We say this apple/honey/peanut butter is poison until we say it's not.

#

Our last night, I was in your apartment before you were. Breath expelled from everywhere. I felt you watching from the corners, hair slicked and shirt tucked. Cigarette burns in the carpet, a shattered dish in the sink. The fucked-up upscale life to which you'd stopped committing. You said you were at work, but you stumbled home hours after quitting time with your pockets inside out and a bag of groceries. *Dinner?* You turned slurped chicken into a kiss. You held a red pepper like a heart ripe for slicing. I sat on your lap and sang, *It took a long time to leave you, Loose Wheel.* That was when the credits should've rolled.

I told you I was getting divorced and had to go home. I left you a key to someone else's house. The sun wouldn't quit exploding. I stashed a hand pump in the glove box and drove miles of dirt roads. Here's the thing: you and I saw hundreds of aquamarine lakes too cold to swim in. Here's the other thing: I was far from home and getting farther. I was at that point where I wanted to separate what was buoyant from what wasn't. I razored off my breasts and sailed them on the oily water. I sank my house key, then drove the long way toward morning.

#

The moral of the story knocked at the door.
The moral of the story can't see very far.
The moral of the story is sure to taste sweet.
The moral of the story will not forsake us.
The moral of the story had not had a happy hour.
The moral of the story was made up with white sheets.
The moral of the story won't get away.
The moral of the story will come to get you.
The moral of the story did no good.
The moral of the story dropped everything.
The moral of the story was pitch dark.
The moral of the story is a fool.
The moral of the story wept bitter tears.
The moral of the story became more and more familiar.
The moral of the story was breaking.
The moral of the story will point the way home.

#

She stores truckfuls of grief in her body. Proves it with scars. Keeps a box of photos and collection notices and custody agreements in her closet.

She's changed her number and locks but we know where she lives and we'll come in uniform with subpoenas and court orders and absolute conviction.

GRANDMA'S HOUSE

By now you know the secret: the girl meets the wolf in the woods, but it doesn't end at Grandma's house. There are lots of girls. Lots of wolves. Some girls aren't girls at all. Some wolves have mortgages and graduate degrees. Only a few are canine, and of those, fewer have shown signs of aggression. You've seen variations on the theme: politically correct, anime, animal rights; the star-studded musical; the ice spectacular. You've tired of certain modern-day updates, the techno-futurescape or the one done in tweets. Gender play is old news. Villains have been redeemed, rehabilitated, and rehashed.

By now you get it: once upon a time never happens once. There are always more ways to tell it.

#

This story has not been rated. It may include some or none of the following: cannibalism, rape, sexual deviancy, kneejerk epiphanies, dream sequences, disturbing archetypes, violence, problematic parallels, feminism, lack of feminism, flashbacks within flashbacks, irresponsible parodies, mixed metaphors, and plagiarism.

#

Now you're ready for a tale. A hero. Here's one.

The wolf and the girl move in together after the girl gets a well-paying job. Let's say she's an analyst. She writes reports and works long hours. She networks. She keeps her finger on the pulse of technology/the economy/the market, but nobody knows what she does. Her friends call her a bean counter. It's a joke, though over the years she finds it difficult to remain a good sport. They're jealous of her shoes, her apartment, her life with the wolf. They all wanted wolves, got sheep instead. They don't have to admit it for it to be true.

It gets to where she's turning down more invitations than she accepts. The wolf wants to know why they never go out anymore. You might call the wolf a social butterfly. He wouldn't take offense. Around the girl's friends, he feels like a celebrity; at home, he's little more than a pet. A kept wolf. He can't remember the last time he's killed anything bigger than a spider.

"Want me to pack you a lunch?" she says one morning.

"What's wrong with our friends?" he responds.

She can't explain. Her friends – and they are all her friends – think it must be so refreshing to be with a wolf. They are always pointing out how willing he is to let her be both breadwinner and conquest. He's not distracted by human contradiction.

They don't consider the details. Like how he shits outside but refuses to pick it up. "Wolves don't care about those things," he says, even though it's in their lease that he not leave waste on the ground, and because she doesn't want to get evicted, she picks it up, which he must know, and she knows he must know, and some days it is all she can do not to say *If you want to live in the woods, go back to the goddamn woods*, but even if she doesn't say it out loud, they are always reacting to its ultrasonic frequency. It's the thing she very loudly doesn't say.

So she picks up his shit because she loves him, or she loves their life, or she loves the fact that she doesn't have to think, right now, about whether or not she loves him or their life. She knows it is a harder life than others. Not as hard as some. History becomes fate. She was destined to marry the wolf because she had married the wolf. In tale after tale, he was there, already home when she arrived.

Fuck the Grimms, she'd thought on her wedding day. Fuck Charles Perrault. They don't know a thing about me and him.

#

You could be the wolf. We don't mean symbolically. We mean, do you eat red meat and know the quickest route home? Are you a top? Do you laugh when you're not supposed to? Have you recently taken a self-quiz to see if you're a) anxious b) attractive c) villainous d) a wolf? Have you pretended to be someone you're not? Can you do voices? Do you eat too much? Have you ever fallen asleep and woken with a rock sewn into your belly?

Ignore that last one.

The girl is harder. She's either an idiot or a genius. One of those types you can't pin down, not even by age. We are the girl, even though some of us are grandmothers and some of us are boys in girls' clothing. We're old-fashioned and deceitful. We've been told not to stray from the path, but we don't heed warnings. We cozy up to strangers and jump into bed with any warm body. If Grandma asks us to strip before the fire, what do we do?

You know what we do. We aren't afraid of being naked, or lost, or eaten.

#

Spoiler alert: we get eaten. It's not like you think.

#

So the girl and the wolf live on the third floor of a six-story building. Halfway between her mother and grandmother. They have balance. They have an origin story they enjoy telling. They have needs that can be met in predictable ways.

Which, as you might expect, isn't enough. The girl feels restless, dissatisfied. There's no Facebook group or Meetup to trade notes with others like her. Wolf-wives tend to be solitary types, or at least they end up that way. Our girl is no longer a girl, anyway, no longer crudely drawn and mutable. She's entered the stage where she gives in to type: career woman, quaffed and preoccupied, plugged-in and opinionated. Her make-up fine-tuned, her comebacks rote. She works for the weekend, but weekends find her pacing the apartment in unflattering yoga pants, flitting on her laptop, washing dishes by hand for no reason. Our Lady of Perpetual Discontent. She considers children because it's the last thing left to do. It's either that or go to an ashram in India. She does a quick search for ashrams, is immediately disenchanted with the pandering to Westerners, does another search for orphanages. She's sure that's not what they're called, but she doesn't know what else to look up. Shelters? A few house wolf pups with the children, capitalizing on the pro-integration zeitgeist, and she zeroes in on them, opening multiple tabs. Was it wrong to treat your pet like a child or your child like a pet? What if you could have both in one package?

She fills out a pre-approval form at a place called Grandma's House. It seems a little sketchy, which is why she likes it. Wolf-wives tend to be risk-takers, or at least they start out that way.

She gets an instant pre-approval, and then her phone begins to ring.

#

And what about the wolf? Did he even want to be a father, and if so, of what? He let the girl choose the apartment, the cellular plan, the wedding date. Breakfast this morning. He put his foot down about which kind of canned chili she bought, but otherwise he let her plan their lives and take the fall whenever something went wrong.

Like the wedding. She'd worn red. And later, after the ceremony and pictures, he'd confessed that the color had bothered him. *I just don't see why we had to reinforce the stereotype,* he'd said, to which she'd replied, *It was just a dress,* and he said, *Pricey dress,* and she said, *You really want to go there?* and to his credit, he'd dropped it. But still. Damage done.

When she insisted that he be responsible for small decisions, like which movie to rent, he'd selected *Christine,* the 1983 horror flick about a car that murders people. The car is named Christine. Christine is sentient and can regenerate herself. The wolf was genuinely hurt when the girl laughed at his choice, and he launched into a tirade about how much he'd given up to live in *her* world, and when she suggested that *her* world was pretty damn comfortable, and that he wouldn't be watching movies at all in *his* world, he sulked in silence for a week.

She picked the movie from then on.

#

We're being careful, aren't we? We've sidestepped wedding night in favor of movie night, and skipped the sex entirely, though few in the old days did that. We'd look like downers to them, prudish and unfunny with our big epiphanic statements about love. We hear her friends unapologetically ask: *how exactly does that work?*

"Well," she says with exaggerated innocence, "when a wolf loves a woman very very much..."

Ha, her friends say. *You're funny.*

Does she even have time for sex? Does working so hard kill her appetite? Her friends spice it up by role-playing wolves. Her friends are all wolves at heart. Pack-minded. Hierarchical. *You must be the alpha,* they tell her.

"We don't use that kind of language," she says.

She doesn't want to picture her friends doing things with men they insist on talking about doing. Human men look like apes to her now. Maybe they always have. She doesn't want to explain the difference, or how, if sex was all that mattered, they'd be perfectly suited.

The girl and the wolf have a healthy and GGG sex life. They are the best they've ever had. You want a peephole into their bedroom? Too bad. Google the sex tape. Read the old stories and watch her throw her clothes into the fire, piece by blessed piece.

She doesn't do that shit anymore.

#

The wolf was due home a half-hour before he arrived. The girl printed her adoption pre-approval form, wondering where he was. Probably out doing wolfy things like slinking and howling, she thought, just before he appeared at the door with two lattes, and then she felt so guilty she blurted out, "We're pre-approved." She flapped the still-warm papers in her hand. "I mean to adopt, I mean I am, I mean I'm sure you could be too, if you wanted," and he said, "What?" and she said, "I feel like I need something more, something bigger than me and you, a connection to life and the universe," and he said, "What?" and she said, "The ashrams were booked." They sat on the couch, knee to knee. She cried, then he cried, then they cried together.

"I want to do this with you," she said, and his pupils swelled.

She could already feel them warping into a new normality. For once they would be like everyone else, smugly ensconced in their own nuclear unit. No one would expect it, but everyone would approve.

She'd never done anything culturally sanctioned from the moment she left her mother's house until now. She worried, briefly, it might dissolve her.

#

See what we did there? Rest assured: she gets eaten, not dissolved. We'll go ahead and put too fine a point on it. The moral of the story is that one mustn't ever read one's own story too early.

"When all the details fit perfectly," Charles Baxter says, "something is probably wrong with the story."

#

Spoiler alert: something is probably wrong with this story.

#

Grandma's House smelled like grandma, that is, the girl's grandma, who'd raised a litter of wolves herself before it was legal, and though her daughter – the girl's mother – had since eschewed that way of life, it was exactly what the girl gravitated towards, once she was old enough to gravitate. Some predilections skip a generation. Or, more typically but also more accurately, her mother's disapproval drove her into the belly of the beast.

The reception area smelled yeasty and doggy, with a tang of rubbing alcohol from the hand sanitizers staggered every two feet across the long front desk. She signed in and sat, then checked her shoes to see if she'd stepped in anything. It'd happened more than once because of the shit-removal debacle, and wouldn't strike the balance of either maternal or paternal, give or take, that she was going for. She felt a drip slide from her bra clasp to her waist and realized she was sweating.

In her purse, folded into a business envelope, was the pre-approval form. She'd been told she didn't need it, but she preferred having a lot of proof of things. She carried ID at all times, as well as her marriage card, her voter registration, and her official membership to the Wolf-Wife Task Force, which offered immediate legal advice in emergencies. She also carried a lipstick-sized bottle of pepper spray, which wasn't technically identification but felt like a version of the same thing.

What we're saying is that she was fully aware of her vulnerability and had armed herself in the most efficient and practical ways of her time. In that respect, her mother had taught her well. *The most dangerous creature of all*, her mother was fond of saying, *is the one you don't notice.*

The innocent-looking toady next to you.

The bacteria in the wolf's teeth, say, instead of the teeth.

#

By now you've got theories. We're game.

Ways people get eaten, other than by talking wolves: real wolves and other nonverbal predators; necrotizing fasciitis, AKA flesh-eating bacteria; proprietor of gingerbread house; post-shipwreck short straw; zombies; own twin; dinner with Mr. Dahmer; oral sex; evil stepmother's soup du jour; transubstantiation; killer tomatoes; guilt/regret/boredom; dystopian society/ancient Greece; Hall & Oates song; dilophosaurus altercation after shutting down park's defenses and attempting to steal dinosaur genomes; wrong place + wrong time.

#

As she waited for her Placement Integration Nurse to lead her back, the bells on the front door dinged and in sauntered a dude. Flannel shirt, unblemished hiking books, full hipster beard: he was as much of an eye roll as she was. He signed his name and took the seat next to her, manspread onto her armrest, reconsidered, and worked a phone out of his back pocket to silence. Looked over at her, away, over again.

"Hate to be the one," he said quietly, almost romantically, "but – XYZ."

"Pardon?"

"Your uh," he pointed at his own crotch in a nonthreatening way, and she glanced down to see her fly was open, a little piece of blouse poking through.

"Jeez." She angled away from him to correct. "Thanks."

"I'd want someone to tell me."

It wasn't in the wolf's nature to notice improprieties. He'd once let her leave the house with the entire side of a complicated blouse unzipped, and she hadn't realized the error until halfway through her workday. On the upside, neither garlic breath nor B.O. offended him.

"You spend months preparing for this," she said, though she hadn't, "and then forget how to dress yourself."

The hipster chuckled. "Good training for motherhood." He glanced at her. "Or whatever."

She let it go. She didn't know what she was training for. She expected that, once she was led into the nursery, the right decision would appear like a portal. If it didn't, she planned to go back to school for fashion design. Or maybe become a volunteer dumpster diver for Green Glean. Maybe she'd quit her job and live in a tent at the mall, call it an art installation. Maybe she'd get a tattoo.

She didn't picture doing any of these things with the wolf, which was problematic, and which was why she was here. This was what she could do with him. If they had a family, it would be something they had.

"Are you, like, here alone?" she started, but the back door swung open and a young woman in bright red scrubs appeared.

"Come on back," she sang. And added, "Both of you."

"Oh," the girl said. "We're not together."

"Yes, you are," the nurse said. "For this part."

The wolf would've come, had he been allowed. The great irony of a place like this was that adult wolves – unless they were service animals – were prohibited. Federal policy. So rather than pace outside while she changed their lives forever, he'd opted to stay home with his ringer on.

Her phone buzzed: a dancing flower emoji from him.

The nurse introduced herself as Nurse Christine. She looked vaguely familiar, but the girl couldn't place her, and this was because Christine had cut and dyed her hair since the last time the two had met, over a decade ago. There was also a context problem happening, like when you see your gynecologist eating a corn dog at the state fair. Not that that's ever happened to us. We remember Christine perfectly. But our hero wouldn't be a hero without adversity, so she'll need a better moment to make the connection.

\#

Spoiler alert: you might've thought we were joking about the sex tape. We'd like to come clean. The girl had bankrolled her year abroad after college by accepting a role in the Big Bad series, before she met the wolf. She's fairly certain neither he nor anyone in her circle knows about it. Her tape is fairly obscure, being well into the series, and for all her friends' talk, they aren't really the sex tape types. She'd quit once her career took off, but she keeps the red cape, laundered and folded, in a drawer in her office. It's a cape, not a hood, and privately she puts a lot of stock in the distinction.

Nurse Christine had a mouth full of corn dog, so to speak, the last time the girl had seen her. In the Big Bad series, the twist is that the girl eats the wolf. Debatable, whether the act is pro- or anti-girl.

#

Nurse Christine led them into a hallway lined with closed doors bisected by windows. Photos and hand-written descriptions of the adoptables framed the doorways, and plaques presented the name of each room – Grandma Jenn's Room, Grandma Chana's Room. Inside each, a woman with an apron and bun knitted in a rocker. Presumably Jenn and Chana, etc., though they weren't old enough to be real grandmas, at least not in the traditional sense. They looked like college kids, and when the girl asked, the nurse mentioned an internship program.

"Ours is a unique facility," Nurse Christine whispered, like a secret. "We find that housing the canids with the homonids makes them a better fit for our families." She pointed at one and then the other of them. "The kiddos grow up understanding pup language, and vice versa. Some of them are quite bonded."

They paused at the window to Grandma Allee's room. Cribs and baskets lined the perimeter, and the walls were decorated with forest decals. Chew toys and rattles cluttered the floor. The girl watched a crawling baby lap from a water dish.

"This might seem like a stupid question," the hipster said, and the girl perked up. She loved it when other people asked stupid questions. "But how do we know which to choose? I mean," he ducked his head and looked up in a photogenic way, "species-wise? Are we supposed to already know?"

Nurse Christine rubbed his back. "We have counseling for that."

The girl wondered why he was here. A distant relative, probably, someone who claimed to have such-and-such percent wolf blood. Or maybe he was gay. No one ever talked about men who married wolves, same-sex or otherwise.

"Can we go in?" the girl said.

"Knock first."

The girl went back to the beginning. Grandma Jenn's Room. She wanted to distance herself from the hipster, to pretend she didn't have the same question he did. She disliked all counseling: marriage, financial, exit. She worried she'd give away some crucial nugget, reveal that her grasp of the world was diluted and mostly poached. The staff here assumed that, at the very least, she wanted to parent, and she even recalled a question on the pre-approval form that spoke to that. She'd hovered over *maybe* before clicking *yes.* She suspected her motives wouldn't stand up to scrutiny.

She entered Grandma Jenn's room: three babies and three pups, all named after '80s pop stars. Paula, Bryan, Belinda. Bon, Boy, Def. Jenn had pink-streaked hair and an apron patterned with cartoon sashimi. Some kind of Gaelic music played from hidden speakers. There was an underlying odor of feces.

The girl checked her shoes again. And her zipper.

"Welcome," Jenn said without pausing her knitting. A baby and a puppy batted the ball of yarn back and forth, while a second puppy watched intently.

"Thanks. I'm just here to –" the girl stopped herself from saying *browse,* but couldn't conjure the appropriate word.

"We encourage observation and interaction," Jenn said, "depending on your comfort level."

"Okay." The girl had no comfort level. She stood for a while, feeling like an intruder, then sat on the floor with her back to the wall. One of the babies sniffed her shoe, and she said, "Hello." The baby dropped a squeaky toy on her knee and stared at her, so she threw it, but the baby's face crumpled and it crawled away. The others in the room watched her warily. She tried to imagine loving one of them but couldn't. It's too soon, she thought. How quickly was one supposed to fall in love with one's own progeny? Did you adopt first, hope for the best? Was there a trial period or return policy? She imagined bringing home something in a kennel or carseat, stashing jars of mashed food in the pantry, going to the park. The night wakings. The way she'd start saying *I have to go home and feed Junior* to get out of obligations. Every available space in her apartment jammed with carriers and apparatuses and appliances. Did a mother ever feel prepared? What if she fell in love and the little one died? What if it was boring or violent or allergic or goth? What if it loved the wolf more than her? What would her mother say if she brought home a wolf? And what would her grandmother say if she brought home a baby?

"Great apron," she said to Jenn.

"Makes me hungry," Jenn said.

The girl gestured to the room. "Do you have any of your own?"

"Someday."

"And –" the girl was aware of the delicacy of the question, though she doubted either the babies or puppies could understand – "which would you pick?"

"I'll have a baby," Jenn said. "No question. This is my first exposure to canids. I'm learning a lot."

"Oh." The girl was sorry she'd asked. She felt like an experiment. People used humans' long relationship with domesticated dogs to justify wolf-human families, but dogs weren't wolves, and studies had found that dogs were more like humans than any other species, including wolves, including even apes, and no one was suggesting anyone marry an ape, though people did sometimes raise chimps as babies with disastrous results.

"But really," Jenn continued, her voice pitching upward – *she knows she said the wrong thing,* the girl thought – "you can't go wrong. These critters are all piles of love, aren't you?" She tousled a baby's curly head.

"My husband's canid," the girl said. "But we never call it that."

"An interspecies family, how wonderful," Jenn said. She sounded indifferent; probably everyone who walked in had the same story. The girl wondered if Jenn ever said anything not pre-programmed. If the ability to knit was a job requirement. If they drilled the grandmas on acceptable vocabulary. She'd once bartended in a place where the manager made the staff recite the mission statement before clocking in, and if you couldn't, you were sent home. *We serve nothing we wouldn't eat ourselves.*

In other words, Grandma's House struck the girl as oddly corporate.

Another baby crawled up and stared at her. She had the urge to poke its forehead, see if it was real. "Do they ever fight?"

The yarn ball tumbled placidly from pup to baby and back.

"There are the usual scuffles," Jenn said. "But very few, considering."

The girl poked the baby.

The baby howled; Jenn yelped and jumped up. "Sorry," the girl said. "I'm not good with kids. I should go."

She stood. The trees on the wall seemed to sway.

"I need you to sign out," Jenn said, but she was busy soothing the baby and the girl slipped from the room without leaving a record of her visit.

#

The girl pushed back into the waiting room and then onto the street. The hipster was propped against the brick side of the building, smoking a pipe. He looked at her guiltily. "You, too?"

She leaned against the wall next to him. "I should get a tattoo."

He pushed up his sleeve and showed her his: some sort of trumpet. "Offspring grow up," he said. "But ink is forever."

"Do you play?"

"I played the French Horn in high school. But this is from Pynchon. The muted post horn?"

"I don't read."

"Me neither." He shrugged. "It's just a tattoo."

A taxi pulled up, wolf in back. For a second, she thought her wolf and instinctively stepped away from the hipster. But this was a wolf from a younger generation, his coat glossy, tongue pierced. She knew not to stare, but she couldn't help watching him climb out of the taxi, all that restrained power, the way her wolf had been when she met him. It wasn't that she wanted to be eaten; it was that she wanted him to choose not to eat her. She wanted to be reminded that, after all these years, it was still a choice.

Other people stared at the wolf, too. He didn't acknowledge any of them, but he startled when the girl sneezed from the exhaust.

"Bless you," the hipster said.

She thanked him. The wolf never said bless you. He never offered her a hand up. He didn't walk her to her car or replace burnt-out light bulbs. He constantly misread her body language. But at the end of the day, when she laid her head in his lap, or buried her face in his thick neck, she forgave all. Their bodies understood each other. It was when either of them opened their mouths that it fell apart.

The front door dinged, and Nurse Christine poked her head out. The hipster hid his pipe behind his leg.

"What are you doing out here?" she said.

The girl collapsed a little. "Having an existential crisis."

"Oh yeah," Nurse Christine said with what sounded like real sympathy. "Those are the worst."

She came all the way out, stood on the other side of the hipster, took a drag off his pipe. It was the smoking that jogged the girl's memory, and she had a flash of Christine in a chrome-colored thong, spread eagle on a wood floor. She flushed, wondered if Christine recognized her, too.

"So existence," Christine exhaled. "Literally, all we've got."

"What's your story?" the hipster said, and the girl braced herself, but Christine just licked her lips and said, "Same as yours. Not enough lives."

They held up the building together in silence.

#

Spoiler alert: Nurse Christine gets fired. But she turns out okay.

#

We found this in an internet search on being eaten alive: "Pain is essentially a signal from the body that something is damaging it. Response strategies can be absolutely different, and they or their absence mean nothing."

#

In one version, the girl fucks the hipster. You saw that coming, right? That's the one where the moral is to stick to your own kind, that similarity trumps difference, and maybe, after all, that's the story people want to hear. How often do the star-crossed lovers make it out unscathed? Who's to say that the pressure of a stigmatized life is forever endurable? Maybe the girl gave up. Maybe the wolf was always destined to lose her. Look at him: right now composing and erasing a text that asks the question point blank. He's no dummy. He doesn't know about the hipster, specifically, but he can feel the girl drifting. He can't decide if she'll be flattered or annoyed by the rom-com nature of: *Have I lost you?*

Yes, she might answer. Or, *No*. Or, *WTF?*

He doesn't send the text.

While he's deciding, she's three streets over in a bathroom stall, telling the hipster how big he is. It's not the first time she's cheated on the wolf, but it'll be the only one she admits, later. The wolf will want to work it out, but in the weeks that follow, their arguments will get increasingly ugly, ultimatums and failed compromises, and finally the image she'll never shake of him standing in the yard with green plastic bags, hunched over his own shit in a last-ditch effort to save the marriage. She'll hate herself for seeing him that way. He's done everything right, though to end it she'll have to say otherwise.

"You don't *do* anything," she'll say, and he'll bravely make a sad little list of the things he did do – "1. Laundry 2. Spiders" – and she'll retaliate with every trite complaint in the book. "You're suffocating me," she'll say. "I've been living a lie." And, since she's not averse to the low blow, "Your kind wouldn't understand."

She doesn't believe most of it. She'll regret it all. The wolf loved her; everyone knows that. But he always gets the shaft. He's too loaded with his own character.

The hipster, on the other hand, smells like sugar cookies. He's barely worth the effort of bending over. We tire of him as fast as she does, get the hell out of there as soon as he's zipped back up.

In another version, the wolf eats the hipster.

In a version we might call the three-way mirror, the wolf eats the girl eats the wolf eats the girl.

In the literary version, the eating is symbolic.

In the sci-fi version, technology eats her.

Her tattoo would've said, *My, what a big tattoo.*

We are all the girls in all the versions, and we've lived out hundreds of thousands of lives, and we are also the same girl, leaning against a building, somewhere between falling in and out of love, acutely aware of the expulsion of potential from each breath as her many lives shrink into one life, and worse, the life she's already lived. It's that hopeless dawning that she's going to keep doing exactly what she's been doing. All the avenues, the aqueducts, the trails to elsewhere dry up. Mirages, the lot of them. People can change, sure, but the girl, this girl, our girl, will not. Her next move has been scripted at birth. She was a metaphor in a past life, and in fraught moments like this one, she knows what a terrible burden that is.

The point is that there are any number of ways for her to be happy, and some versions of the story allow for that through no fault or brains or predisposition of her own, and the point is that a wolf is never just a wolf, nor a girl just a girl, but for the purposes of our story, morals are always moral, though they can be absolutely different, and they or their absence mean nothing.

She will never have the hipster's hipster baby, born with a three o'clock shadow and its own indie playlist. She'll never go on birth control and take his last name and buy a ukulele. She'll never speak to Christine again. She'll never get the tattoo. She'll never stay with the wolf so they can celebrate the staying, stave off the inevitable ending, achieve that stop-time effect that substitutes for closure. What we're saying is that she'd like us to finish the story here, having granted her the twin pearls of tragedy and wisdom. She has suffered and grown. She's becoming more human by the minute.

That's about to end. Do you know why?

Because we're not in the business of granting wishes.

Because we promised you a better ending.

Because Angela Carter said the girl was nobody's meat, but Angela Carter isn't here. This story does not belong to anyone. And the girl isn't really a girl.

We told you so. This story may contain broken promises. It may contain traces of allergenic foods, chemicals tied to disease, compounds impossible on earth, classified information. It may lack resolution. You've been warned and warned and warned again. We could stand in your path with a pair of red flags, but it wouldn't do the trick. Your carriage is still going to be robbed. Your SUV is still going to flip. The curtains will catch fire and the frat party will proceed as planned. The first day the girl goes back to work after moving into her own place, a coworker will announce she's pregnant. The girl will offer her warmest congratulations because she knows the coworker's fortune is just another version of her own. Her job is to live out this version to the best of her ability, turn what's been given into a satisfying resolution. She doesn't believe us when we tell her she'll be eaten.

She won't listen. *We are your history and your future*, we say, but she keeps going as if she owns the present. As if she's the only girl who ever lived. Look at her: she's going to take you home next.

NOBODY UNDERSTANDS YOU LIKE US

We encouraged her to get the dog. Not that we take responsibility, because we don't, and the word we used was *puppy,* by which we meant a retriever for the kids or a terrier she could train to wave bye-bye, but she's one of those sanctimonious types hell bent on salvaging wrecks, so of course she went to the pound, and of course she started with Death Row, and of course she chose an animal no one else wanted. That no one wanted *for good reason* is our point, but she didn't ask our advice. Never mind that we shared twenty feet of chain link in the back. Never mind the howling. We'd have told her to avoid anything high-pitched or hairy, no googly eyes or missing legs, nothing elderly or special needs, and okay, pick an ugly one if you have to, but for god's sake, don't bring home the animal that belongs in the woods.

We might not have thought to say, specifically, don't bring home a wolf.

What she did was she brought home a wolf.

Claimed it was a mixed-breed husky, but no amount of paperwork could convince us it was domesticated at all. It didn't walk, it slunk. Army-crawled across the sidewalk. Patchy fur and beady eyes, silver tuft between its shoulders that stood up like a dorsal fin. The leash like an insult around its neck.

The day she brought it home, one of us whispered, *That thing has definitely eaten Grandma.*

The Neighborhood

Swear to god, right then every bird in the neighborhood went silent.

We didn't confront her right away. Poor thing was a divorced mom, no family or friends, and if she'd made a single good decision in her life, we didn't know about it. Her ex- was a real condescending type who once stole a snow shovel off our porch and replaced it with an inferior snow shovel. We were glad she'd gotten rid of him. We wanted her to heal and be the good neighbor we knew she could be, inviting us over for dinner and whatnot, the kids clinging to our legs when we walked in...we didn't have children, but we thought we'd be good godparents, though we weren't entirely sure what the job entailed, and anyway, we weren't trying to jump the gun on the relationship, just that she was exactly the kind of lost soul we liked to befriend. We had a whole bevy of lost souls in our rotating potluck, and they always brought the best cocktails.

We hoped if she ever stopped moping she'd see how she didn't need anyone else because we could mow her grass in the summer, and bring chicken soup if the kids were sick, and give her a cup of sugar if she was – well, she wasn't the cookie-making type, but you know what we mean – and that's the kind of neighborhood we wanted to live in. We could've taught the puppy to balance a biscuit on its nose, or -- we're not opposed to thinking big – to do magic tricks like in that video that went viral. We could've been famous, and not in the way we are here, now, talking to you.

She was suffering. You hear stories about mothers who crack, and you always wonder about the bystanders, the family, the *neighbors*, and there we were, watching her unravel and telling ourselves we had to do something. We're not heartless. We worried about the children and also our property values. There had been a number of car prowls and a problem with graffiti, and we're not saying her oldest son was responsible, but we'd caught him in the alley more than once. So yes, we called Child Services. And yes, they did a home visit. And when she asked if we knew who'd narked on her, and when she explained how *that little curve ball* was going to affect her custody battle, and when her tone got too snippy for us, we suggested she get a puppy.

But she brought home the wolf, and then instead of buying dog biscuits, we were stocking up on pepper spray to keep the thing from lunging at us every time we returned the gym balls her kids whiffed over the fence.

But now we're getting ahead of ourselves.

Those kids were trouble, it's true, but we admit to not entirely thinking through the whole Child Services thing.

#

The day she brought home the wolf, we were at her door within the hour, holding the gift we'd made, a mug for her and a matching water dish for the puppy. Her eyes slid from one of us to the other.

"Greg," she said. "Linda."

"Hi, Jamie," we said.

She smiled. Well, smirked. Difference between laughing at and laughing with, as Mr. Fletcher, our high school band director, used to say. Band kids get picked on, which was why we stuck together. *You should get married,* he told us. *Nobody understands you two like you do.*

The wedding was perfect. We said our vows in unison.

That was almost thirty years ago. Sometimes, when the rotating potluck lands at our house, we break out the clarinets and play our wedding march from memory. We can also do the fight song and national anthem, and we take requests when our friends remember to bring sheet music. Jamie came once, but she drank too fast and clogged the toilet, and when this one guy, Clark, who always said what everybody else was thinking, asked her what she did in her free time, she pounced. "Time is always free," she said, raising a shaky glass. "When we stop believing that, we cease to be human." The glass tipped, and the wine went everywhere.

She declined all invitations after that, even though we told her the stain came right up.

We appreciated that she thought about what it meant to be human. When we got philosophical, our friends told us to lighten up, and that was disappointing because of the unexamined life not being worth it or whatever.

The day she brought home the wolf, Jamie stood in her doorway waiting for us to say what we wanted, so we started in, volleying back and forth and interrupting each other how we do: *congrats on the new pet, is it really a husky? big enough to be a guard dog, must be some kind of zoo reject, not going to lie, looks like a flipping wolf!*

"A wolf?" she said. "I guess a little."

Not judging! Not criticizing! But what's the return policy because it seems dangerous, frankly, and we're worried about you and the kids, which, where are the little hellions by the way, hellions in a good way of course, they upstairs?

"With their father." She slumped against the doorframe. "He gutted me in court."

We gasped. She frowned.

"It wasn't because of you," she said. "He dragged in my whole personal life."

We knew what that meant. A visit from child services was nothing compared to her personal life, which, truthfully, we didn't approve of either. Her new friends were worse than her ex-. We say friends, but they were her lovers or whatever you call it. They didn't make polite company or have real names. The last one went by Al, but we called her the witch doctor because she carried this old-fashioned medical bag for a purse and wore a fur coat – we're put off by the whole business, so we don't even want to speculate – mink? – and once we asked our friends what everyone thought was in that huge bag, if it was herbs or spells or body parts on ice, but Clark just said it was probably booze, and where was the fun in that?

The witch doctor is the one you heard about, but there were others. One had a yappy dog she kept in her car all night, parked on the street in front of our house, so we left a note on her windshield that we didn't appreciate the dog's noise, and the next day our lawnmower got stolen.

Another one kept knives in her glove compartment. Don't ask how we know. Not pocket knives, either; more in the category of weaponry. *Deadly weapons,* as Kip Clipson, the host of *America's Likeliest Criminals,* says, and if we're being honest, there were striking similarities between Jamie's new friends and America's likeliest criminals.

It was like Jamie needed to love things that were hard to love. Maybe that was her talent. Maybe that was her downfall. It was definitely her downfall, but maybe it was what she needed to survive. Like she dealt with pain by summoning it. If not pain, then danger. Maybe she thought she was being proactive, inoculating herself against real tragedy.

She wasn't. But we admire her for the thought, if that was her thought.

#

Is it wrong to say we expected better because she was a mother? We'll put it this way: Jamie was no victim. We're not saying she got what she deserved, but we want you to know it's not like it sounds. She took unnecessary risks. She fostered tendencies in herself she would've done well to suppress. We thought a puppy might convince her to act less like a sex-crazed lunatic. We hope you don't mind if we're blunt about that. It's not like we *want* to say these things. We liked Jamie. She was good people, as Mr. Fletcher used to say. She was solid.

But she left her windows open when she and her lovers were going at it – they called it *fucking*, if you want to know, and we didn't think that was appropriate in a house with children – and we don't think she even owned curtains.

Sometimes, listening to them, we'd kiss each other and promise never to be mad. Sometimes we got a little frisky ourselves and wondered what would happen if we let loose like that. We didn't really want to find out, just that they seemed so grateful to be alive and young and naked, and don't get us wrong, we love each other, but we're not young anymore, and we certainly never walked around naked. We've also never had to call the cops on each other, so there you go. It was like living next door to this great movie. Maybe it makes your life seem smaller, but once it's over, you're grateful to be back in your car and headed somewhere familiar.

Jamie never knew where she was going. She needed stability. We thought that even if a puppy didn't help, it couldn't hurt. Boy were we wrong about that.

To be fair, she didn't get a puppy. We want to be very clear about that. We never suggested she get a wolf.

#

We told Jamie we were sorry about the custody thing, and she invited us in for tea, and we would've gone in, we absolutely would've, if the wolf hadn't right then skulked up behind her. Fixed us in its evil gaze, tongue lolling. It looked at our necks and salivated. She'd tied a red bandana around its neck, which she took in one hand while she stroked its back with the other. Its expression didn't change or soften. Just meeting its eyes rearranged your soul.

We told her we didn't want to intrude, that we'd talk another time about the wolf.

She smirked again. It was hard not to take offense. "You really think my dog is a wolf." Like she was making note of it.

We backed off the porch, calling our goodbyes from the sidewalk. Jamie pet the wolf hypnotically, muttering, "Goodbye, neighbors."

We tried to talk to her about the wolf on three other documented occasions, but she refused to listen. We've been asked why we didn't call Animal Control, but you have to understand that the thing *came from Animal Control*. It's not like vigilante justice is in our natures. We were band kids. We preferred dinner parties to stakeouts.

We even called our realtor, Sue Singleton, and she did a walk-through but advised us to hold out until spring. "I'd call someone about that dog next door," she said when she left. "It's real off-putting."

We started unlatching Jamie's gate. That's our confession. Maybe it wasn't right, but we felt trapped. We wanted the wolf gone, and we didn't care how it happened.

Meanwhile the thing with Jamie got worse. The witch doctor was there whenever the kids were not, and we'd seen Jamie throw the witch doctor's clothes on the lawn, and we'd seen her lay in the snow while the witch doctor tried to convince her to come inside, and we'd seen her drink a whole bottle of vodka and then vomit off the porch, and we knew she was falling apart. Domestic violence is wrong, and we were pretty sure Jamie was getting the brunt of it. It made us jumpy and exhausted. We never knew when they might have an outburst. Once the witch doctor pounded on our door, and when we didn't answer, she waved her hands around like she was either casting a spell or swatting bugs, but we were pretty sure it wasn't bugs.

"Perverts," she yelled. "Stay off our property." Which was a weird thing to say since it wasn't her property, and all we'd done was politely knock and inform Jamie that we'd seen the wolf stalking somebody's cat across from the Dairy Queen two blocks over.

Before she left, the witch doctor kicked a pot of our begonias off the porch. Jamie was over sweeping terra cotta shards before we could call the police, so we didn't call them, though in retrospect, we should have.

"Sorry about that." Jamie wore the red bandana around her head. "It's been hard."

We kept it short: *You deserve better.*

"I know," she said, nodding, but we could tell she didn't.

Later, Jamie and the witch doctor walked to the ravine at the end of our street and stayed down there a long time. Hours. When they returned, Jamie was wearing the fur coat, and they had the wolf back on its leash. Her ex- dropped the kids off that evening, and the witch doctor made a huge meal that they all ate in the dining room like a regular family. Jamie set out a bowl of food for the wolf, but it looked like it'd just as soon eat her face.

Something bad is going to happen, we said to each other. Jamie's problems had become our problems. We talked about what we needed to do. We agreed that nobody was going to help us, but we were in this together.

We pulled out one of those weekly sales fliers, folded around an ad for a tent sale at Gun World, and decided to go together.

\#

We know what this sounds like. It sounds fake, right? The wolf, the witch doctor? It sounds like we're making this up to get on TV.

We'll take a lie detector, if you have one.

\#

117

The marquee outside Gun World advertised training classes and party rentals. We browsed the pink and orange Swiss Army pens in the tent out from before heading inside. The place was packed. A guy in a white button-down swiped our driver's licenses at the door and directed us to a waiting area, where a girl in an identical button-down shook our hands. "I'm Brittany," she said. "Is this your first visit?"

We nodded. Brittany wore a lot of mascara. She told us she was a psych major at Eastern and had four older sisters, which explained the mascara. She listened attentively to our story, frowning like she was used to hearing bad news.

"Nuisance animals compose a large chunk of our business," she said. "We know the value of a peaceful home." She folded her hands at her chest. "I'm a yoga instructor here, too."

Here? we said. *How wonderful and surprising!* We asked what we should do about the wolf, although we called it a dog. We didn't want to alarm her.

"I can't advise any particular course of action," she said. "But I can show you some options."

We told her that options were exactly what we needed her to show us.

She led us to a roped-off section where demo weapons hung on the wall like athletic shoes. They had names: Happy Ending, Last Resort, Old-Fashioned. One of us modeled the First Timer in a three-way mirror while the other compared Hustler Pro to Hustler Comfort. We eliminated anything too complicated or cheap. Brittany was encouraging but discerning, talking us out of the flashy Rorshach and the nostalgic Western. She recommended the Problem Solver for our needs, and we appreciated the ease of its point-and-shoot operation, as well as the hand-crafted holster. Brittany guaranteed our satisfaction and signed us up for a marksmanship class on Mondays and her own Yoga for Stress Reduction class on Wednesdays.

"It's for every body type," she said as we left.

The Neighborhood

On Mondays we learned how to aim and fire, and on Wednesdays, we meditated on a world where our problem no longer existed. Brittany wore a headset and asked us to imagine how it would feel to live in a stress-free world. She asked us to consider what we could do to eliminate the stressors in our lives. We peeked at each other and the cross-legged people around us, an older woman in sweats, a lanky man breathing loudly. We pictured them solving problem after problem like superheroes.

We appreciated how the class increased our ability to empathize.

At first, the presence of the Problem Solver really did seem to solve our problem. Jamie bought a padlock for the gate, and the witch doctor built this elaborate doghouse in the backyard. She had the kids out there hammering and painting and putting little candy-striped curtains in the windows. Jamie put down mulch in the front yard, even planted a couple of hot pink Gerber daisies. We would've picked something less ostentatious, but we were glad she was finally trying to fix the place up.

We felt okay, and even went ahead with our night of the rotating potluck. That was when we brought out the Problem Solver for the first time.

No, that was you. I never would've done that.

Clark said, "That's frightening," but everyone else seemed impressed. You pointed it out the window at Jamie's house, where the wolf was standing in the window, staring at us as usual. The rest of us laughed nervously until you pulled back the hammer. "Play dead," you said.

The beast stared, unmoved.

"It's not loaded," I said, and you said, "Yes, it is."

You dropped your arm, the Problem Solver by your thigh. Said you needed to take a shower.

I said, "Right now? In the middle of the party?"

You raised the gun and pointed it at me.

Our friends tuttered around, *come on now* and *that's not funny* and they poured more wine and made jokes – *tough guy, eh?* – but they could tell I was shaken. You cracked a smile, finally, and said, "Just teasing."

But you sort of said it to the room, not to me.

Then you went upstairs and took a shower.

Later that night, you climbed on top of me, and I could've sworn your eyes glowed. We did it every night that week. Can we say that? It's true. You smacked my behind once. You'd never done that before.

I thought you said you liked it.

I never said I didn't like it.

#

We were so caught up in each other, we ignored what was going on next door, which is a shame because the next week was when all hell broke loose.

We've traced it to the doctor's bag. Seemed that Jamie, like the rest of us, was curious about what was in it. So she snooped, and whatever she found upset her. We heard them before we saw them. We were walking back from the Dairy Queen, where you'd put my hand in your pocket, and I'd felt the Problem Solver there. I hadn't known you'd brought it, but I kissed you right there on the sidewalk.

"You guys are so cute," a girl watering her lawn told us.

My hand was still in your pocket when we heard the yelling. We knew right away who it was.

"That's private property," the witch doctor barked.

"You lied to me," Jamie yelled.

And so on.

We weren't sure what Jamie had found, but there was a skirmish on the lawn, and at one point Jamie dumped the bag. We got a glimpse of ripped envelopes and tiny liquor bottles before the witch doctor scooped everything back up.

"You bitch," the witch doctor yelled.

Something was going to happen. We could feel it in the air, even before Jamie's son came outside with the wolf. Jamie told him to go back inside, but he picked up a handful of mulch and threw it at her. Hard as he could, right at her head. The wolf jumped around like it was delighted, then it broke free of the leash and leapt right for Jamie's throat.

We could say we only meant to scare them. That's what people say about situations like this. But that would be a lie. We felt calm. Our blood pressure was normal. We didn't want to scare anybody. We wanted to save Jamie.

We took the gun from our pocket.

We always wondered what kind of person we'd be under pressure, and now we knew.

We were flipping amazing. The car prowls stopped after that.

We knew right what to do. Didn't we? Didn't we know exactly what to do?

We did.

And our aim! Blam: problem solved.

Shout out to Brittany at Gun World.

The poor kids, though. They were traumatized for a good long while, though we're sure they're okay by now, or at least we haven't heard otherwise. The thing we'll remember forever, though, is how Jamie held that damn wolf after it died. Everyone froze at the explosion of the gun, and it was like nobody wanted to move again to see what damage was done. The witch doctor held her bag like a shield to her chest. We never saw her again after that.

The wolf's head was blasted open, but Jamie, god bless her, crawled over and gathered that creature in her arms like he was her baby. Stroked its horrible side. Buried her face in its fur. That woman – she generated hope like a force field. Rejected the label *vicious dog* to the end, though that was the official verdict.

We never could explain to her that she didn't have to deal with all that transmutation of pain. We heard she moved into an apartment complex with a gated entry and no-pet policy.

Our new neighbors are a young couple in some buzzword science field we can never remember, bookish and waifish, the kind of people who reminded us of ourselves just starting out, before houses became things to stage, lists of interchangeable amenities and spin. Before we learned how to spray paint and spot clean. The day they moved in, the sun was setting behind the house in a way that covered the roof in light and made it seem holy, like the end of a movie. The trees were still as cardboard.

Welcome to the neighborhood, we said.

THE NEIGHBORHOOD

The wire children move independently and have recognizable faces. They can learn, though the pace of their development would be considered delayed in flesh children. They are LtL, Learning to Learn. We are all LtL, even the mentors, who are not above botching an order, as when they failed to predict the wire children's "limbs" would shred clothes faster than the budget could handle. The wire children have no genitals, not even "genitals," but we are expected to refer to them as *he* and *she* and never *it* because we are all Body Positive and Pro-Nudity in our Neighborhood, which, by the way, is what the mentors call this collection of cabins and mock businesses we accepted in exchange for prison time. The mentors discourage words like *compound* or even *camp*, despite the fenced perimeter, despite the forest outside the fence, despite the fact that we don't really know where we are.

Wherever you go, the mentors are fond of saying, there you are.

Wherever you are, we are fond of saying. There you go.

The wire children age without growing, and we're pretty sure they're incapable of sexual reproduction, but thinking or discussing things like that is frowned upon, even when, as Carmen once pointed out, they're relevant.

I want to know, she'd said, if we're dealing with humanoids or robots or what.

The mentors responded that the wire children were neither humanoids nor robots, and also that they'd brief us on what was or wasn't relevant.

We're going to miss Carmen.

She claims she's going public as soon as she gets out, that there's a loophole in the gag order we sign upon release. We all have to sign it, whether we're court-ordered or volunteer. So far, there's only one volunteer, a certified Support Mama, but since she reports to the mentors, none of us tell her anything. We are here for science, not to compete, but still. We all want to win.

If it's true, Carmen's release will be the first of its kind. But we're not buying it yet. She hasn't done a fraction of her time. A couple of lightweights before her left due to bad behavior, but they went back into the system. Carmen says she's going out free and clear, or so they promised.

Carmen also thinks she's getting her kids back, so we know she's full of shit.

Still, she's nothing if not convincing. In the days leading up to her alleged release, she has half of us picturing her yukking it up on daytime TV and being interviewed by the local news. And the other half hoping, because we can't stand not to, that it's true what she says about getting back her kids.

#

The wire children look a little like sculptures and a little like planters. They're uncomfortable to handle but not dangerous, except on accident. In direct sunlight, their wires get hot enough to burn. They dislike being alone but complain that being with other wire children gives them indigestion. They're clingy and sharp. We are invited to report any injuries we sustain without concern for how such reports would *severely* hinder the study's progress. We have twelve-part First Aid kits in our bathrooms, but Carmen's the only one who can sew a stitch with any skill. If she goes, we'll be left to scar.

Today we're waiting to hear about Mallory's request to throw Carmen a goodbye party, which will confirm or negate the rumor about her release. Third Variable time, off the record and away from the wire children, is rarely approved because requests are numerous and the Neighborhood needs to maintain internal validity. Large-group Third Variable time is not permitted, though we keep trying. Being away from us upsets the wire children, who insist they're capable of emotion. We're not so sure, but there's no reliable test. They might be faking it, which would make them either sociopaths or more autonomous than we'd like to believe.

The mentors have been uncharacteristically quiet about Mallory's request.

We pass the day, as we do most days, in our cabins, which are too small for more than a visitor or two at a time. The cabins circle the courtyard, windows and doors facing inward, in identical layouts: two tiny bedrooms, a corner kitchen with attached toilet, a playroom. Mamas' Rooms have lacey pink curtains on windows that don't open and vases of fake daisies glued to the dressers where we store folded stacks of Mama scrubs. Our bedroom doors lock at nine every evening. The wire children don't have doors. They have plastic mattresses and cork floors and sturdy, donated toys. They are learning how to sleep, but they don't need sleep; they're learning how to play, but the toys wind up mutilated or speared on some appendage that's sprung free, a phenomenon that's so common we have a name for it: the Toy Kabob. The mentors allow us to be playful like this as long as it doesn't impact the study.

We can visit each other if we do it one at a time. We try to keep tabs, make sure no one's losing their shit. No phones for us, but a '70s-style intercom connects the cabins and the Switchboard, which mentor-trainees staff 24-hours a day.

The intercom resembles a radio with a series of dials on a brown speaker. We are permitted only to adjust the volume because, early on, some of the Mamas used the intercoms to develop inappropriate relationships with mentor-trainees. Now they record all conversations, and they put the nanny cams in plain sight on the ceilings. Zee thinks the cameras mean we're part of a reality show, but Zee is the resident conspiracy theorist, and Sarah, the resident hacker, has debunked this particular theory.

The outside world knows about us, but we know less about it every day. Susanna was our sole off-site connection until she went AWOL. She was a Spokesmama and Floater – not a mentor, not really part of the study – and she attended fundraising events alongside the mentors, who used her to field delicate questions about our psychological states, and it was during one of these galas that she disappeared. We miss her coming around to collected data, and we miss probing her for details about how people dressed these days, what foods they ate, what celebrities they gossiped about. We wouldn't have even known about the protesters if it hadn't been for Susanna.

Now that she's gone, each of us thinks we should be the next Spokesmama. We guess at the script and practice our answers for someday. Susanna was no better or smarter or sneakier than us. We can imagine the moment she realized no one was watching. The first step away, waiting for alarms to ring or police to swarm. The unbelievable quiet.

We imagine her now as in the end of a movie: sunglasses and chaise lounge. Handsome dude calling her by a fake name. We all have fake names at the ready.

You there, we say, go wherever.

Free and clear.

#

Tonight, as always, we log on to the Neighborhood Network within five minutes of putting the wire children to bed, and rate our degree of mother-child attachment: low, moderate, high, or profound. Most of us haven't reached moderate. None of us has reached profound. This isn't the fault of the wire children, since they're nothing like the children we want. Attaching to them is supposed to be difficult. That, as we understand it, is the whole point of the study.

Sometimes we try to figure out the scientific questions that govern our lives here, i.e., can bad mothers be taught to be good? Or maybe, can we be incentivized to bond? To love? Susanna said that, when the mentors addressed the more sensitive donors, they pitched the study as a form of rehabilitation. That sounds like a sick joke to us, since we've already lost our kids.

Anyway, we're only guessing. None of us has more than a cursory understanding of the science behind this.

The mentors post our attachment scores on a web forum, along with FAQs and things they call Mandatory Thought Experiments, which are like unanswerable questions we are supposed to answer. 1) Is it possible to successfully parent an unlovable child? 2) If so, what would "success" look like?

Tonight, just for fun, they've added a third: 3) What advice would you give Carmen for returning home?

This is how we know her release is real.

Understanding circulates the ring of cabins, all of us in our rockers with computers in our laps, the third question reflected in our eyes when we lift them to the windows. The courtyard beams with collective dawning. It's all we can see.

On the web forum, the first pieces of advice appear in the form of meek encouragement. *You got this, Mama!* and *You're strong!* to which the mentors reply, *Practice authenticity.* Which means quit lying. Our Neighborhood motto is *Keep promises, but not secrets.* We're supposed to tell the truth at any cost, which means that if a wire child asks if he's ugly, and he is, we have to tell him so. If we say we're going to kill them, even as a figure of speech, we have to kill them. That's the rule, though if any of us knew how to kill them, the study might be over by now.

We pause, trying to figure out how to say to Carmen what the mentors don't want us to say, which is, *Run like hell. Don't look back. Disappear.*

Follow Susanna.

There aren't many free-and-clear fantasies available to us, since our families and friends, such as they were, have disowned us. Our crimes were on the news; our names are known. But Susanna did it. We want Carmen to do it, too, just so we're sure it can be done.

Go wherever, we want to say. Just go.

We choose our words more carefully. The mentors want the truth, but they want it to be usable. *Concentrate on moving forward*, someone writes, and we wait to see if the mentors will allow it, which they do.

Set parameters, someone else writes, advice that's both crucial and impossible. Carmen's that unlucky sort who's good at doing time. Here, she follows each rule to the letter, hits every curve ball out of the park. A textbook success case. It's the jittery, zigzag outside world she can't navigate.

The wire children are as varied in their habits as flesh children, but they are more destructive, as when Leslie's high-energy twins destroyed a dozen plastic mattresses in the course of a month. For comparison, Carmen's kid still has her original. The wire children don't need food or sleep, but we provide both anyway. We're rated on our nurturing abilities but also our firmness. Carmen is the first to post her daily log, and the only one to catch the seven o'clock Pro-Hour of Non-Feed TV. By the time the rest of us turn on the tube, our selections are limited to mentor-approved relaxation channels like Meditation Journeys Through Safe Spaces and Kittens Engaged in Gentle Play. Non-Feed TV, which is basic cable, is supposed to motivate us to sustain a smooth bedtime routine, but all it ever does is give Carmen a superiority complex.

We suspect the mentors went easy on her; we get the feeling they want her gone. We all know what she did to her real kids. Reducing her sentence seems questionable unless the mentors are up to something, which they always are. We hypothesize. Leslie thinks she fucked her way out. Zee says it's all to stir up controversy among the rest of us. Patty says Carmen was dragging down the study – too businesslike, her achievements never tainted by a whiff of unwieldy real emotion. And Mallory, who's been hopelessly and baldly in love with Carmen from the beginning, weeps and calls Carmen her hero.

Whatever the case, the mentors have to know that the rest of us will follow Carmen's lead, tank the study in hopes of getting out. Maybe they underestimate us. Maybe they think the rest of us actually care.

Maybe they think any of us are here because of science.

#

After we've logged our answers, the mentors green-light vacancies in twelve cabins for the Farewell Party – not exactly large-group Third Variable time, but as close as we've ever gotten. The lucky doors open, and the chosen ones marvel at how different night feels when you're in it. The rest of us have mentally mapped the Neighborhood and can picture it as if we were there. To the south, the handful of outbuildings clustered in darkness like set pieces that switch on at designated times. To the north, the mentors' trailers illuminating their own gravel pads. Beyond, the electric fence topped with prison-issue barbed wire. A single gate for both entrance and exit to the service road that leads into the forest. All told, more secure and less cushy than the protestors think. Leslie heard it was once a trappers' camp.

Third-Variable events are held at Mama Loca's, the on-site cantina where those of us who aren't sober-mamas or on their scheduled cleanse can order Margaritas with a splash of real tequila. We eat massive amounts of chips, and the drinkers quickly get slushy and say things they're not supposed to.

Patty says her oldest is turning into a real bitch.

Sarah has discovered she can pick up an unlocked Wifi network if she stands her wire child near the modem.

Zee says they're spiking our food with anti-psychotics.

Leslie claims she caught a mentor-trainee in her bedroom after hours, but we know Leslie, and we're betting that was a consensual arrangement.

And Carmen says, I don't think any of us realize how fucked up this all is.

She looks terrified. She doesn't fully understand what's happening to her either. Her cabin is pristine, ready to be vacated, and her wire child has already been rehomed to an off-site foster family, which Zee says is code for the lab. Carmen is still in her Mama scrubs, but she's reverting to old habits before our eyes, dialing up her accent, fisting her hands. Strapping on the armor.

We follow, in solidarity. Bitch, we say, you gonna fuck shit up out there!

She raises her chin, the softness in her voice bleeding out. You know it, she says. Get your lazy asses out next.

Don't go royal on us, we say, though we're pretty sure she won't. Carmen is going back to the same shithole she came from. She knows it, and we know it. But there's no sense in dredging it up now.

Instead we talk about our wire children, how they won't play together at the on-site playground, how we are trying and failing to love them. Carmen is quiet, and we leave her alone, until finally she says, Dang, you know Blissa cried when they took her away? Man, she really cried.

We are permitted to name the wire children, but not to give them human names. There are no Marys or Jamals in our Neighborhood. All names and nicknames go through an approval process, and violations are curtailed swiftly. We worry so much about violations that we only call the wire children by name when necessary.

We know Blissa cried, and our wire children know too. They'd asked us tough questions before bed, which we were pained to answer honestly. They said, Where is Carmen going? and Why doesn't she want to stay? and Are you going to go away too?

We said: Hush. Forget about Carmen. She was a shitty mom.

We're surprised by any emotion the wire children elicit, and when it happens, we sort of congratulate the mentors in our heads. Which, they've explained, is exactly what they don't want us to do.

But we want to succeed here, we tell them.

We are so grateful to be here, we say.

This is a sure-fire way to get the mentors to scowl and end the session. After Susanna ran off, they realized that most of what we tell them is bullshit.

There you go, we say. Whatever.

We tell Carmen to rename herself Blissa in homage, cut her hair and wear glasses, start at the bottom. If anyone can sweet talk her way out of a background check, it's her.

Just don't forget us, we say, knowing that forgetting us is exactly what Carmen needs to do.

Maybe I'll be a nanny, Carmen says, which is the kind of joke we never say out loud. We laugh so hard it must horrify the mentors who are watching.

#

In the morning, Carmen's gone. The mentors call us via intercom to put our wire children down for naps at noon and meet in the courtyard. The wire children never nap except when the mentors need to make an announcement, which means they're going to shake things up. We huddle on the lawn, which is really turf so it requires no upkeep, shivering in our flip-flops and Mama scrubs. The only individuality we are permitted is how we wear them: too tight, off-the-shoulder, balled at the navel, rolled into shorts. The mentors are always asking us how we feel about our bodies. They expect us to be grateful because our meal plans keep us trim and sober, and most of us have never been either. But the mentors have mistaken us for the kind of women who give a good goddamn about their waistlines. Carmen said the first thing she was going to do when she got out was chase a bag of Doritos with another bag of Doritos.

To be fair, it doesn't matter if we like our new bodies or not. We're criminals and test subjects, not soccer moms on some self-improvement retreat.

The mentors pile out of their van and stand Red Rover-style before us, shoulder to shoulder. Before this, we'd pictured scientists clean-shaven and middle-aged, holding beakers in lab coats. But the mentors look more like a convention of nerds and serial killers. Beards and cardigans and predatory smiles, a couple of fidgety women with bad posture. We note that the head guy, Harry, has come. The one other time we've seen him was at our arraignments, so his presence is a big deal. He's the kind of guy who can pass for grandfatherly: thinning hair, cleft chin, bulletproof sense of entitlement. That diminishing gaze, that sanguine ruthlessness. We love and hate him without trying to do either.

He steps forward, casual, but frowning like a wounded kid. *I'm perplexed*, his face says before he speaks, and whether we want to or not, we're wondering how we can fix the problem.

I'm a scientist, he begins, flattering us with the notion that anyone would mistake him for one of us. He continues: I'm not in show biz. My interest is in that complex machine you're all carrying around with you.

He gives us a moment, then taps his head. Then says, The brain, to make sure we got it.

The brain! – he's in full lecture mode now, arms up, swaying on his feet – It's the most complex thing in the entire universe. By far the most mysterious. Why do we love? Why do we stop loving? Questions that have been the purview of religion and art for centuries, but which have only recently come under scientific scrutiny. You all, you're astronauts. You're deep sea divers. You are the explorers of the new world. I know that. *We* know that...

He sweeps down the line of mentors with his arm. They beam at us, their ragtag band of unlikely astronauts. Then Harry gestures behind him with the other arm, open-handed, pushing away the noise of everyone outside our gated, holy nation.

...but *they* don't. And what *they* tell me is that I've got a P.R. problem on my hands. What do I care about P.R.? I say. This isn't reality television! This isn't a docu-drama! But Harry, they tell me – you're being judged in the court of public opinion. And...

He stops, shakes his head in disgust.

...who funds these projects? That's right. The public. And the public, god bless 'em, would rather see you packed into an overcrowded correctional institution than charting new territory with me. So.

He turns to the mentors, says it again: So. What do we *do*?

Hunches over the last word like it's giving him a cramp. Turns back to us, holds up what we mistake for a peace sign.

We do two things, he says. The first is easy. Publicity. We show them our Neighborhood. We let them see how valuable our work is, how it's all kosher, a win-win partnership between cognitive research and the penal system. I'm talking about a commercial. A commercial? Yes. Something *they* can see. Something calming and affirming. That's number one.

And the second thing?

He smiles. We remember that smile. At our arraignments, it promised relief, leniency, compassion. We all pled guilty, even Patty, who didn't do what they accused her of.

This time he's not promising anything.

He says: The second thing we show them is results.

A couple of the mentors-in-training squirm. The seasoned ones stare straight ahead. They're all students working on degrees, which they've told us about minimally. They've been invasive but respectful; they are cultivating their bedside manners. They always re-introduce themselves and ask questions about things they clearly know the answers to. They're stiff but transparent. When something is a test, they let us know it's a test.

We get the impression that's all about to change.

Harry steps back so Leslie's mentor can step forward to dispense the new protocol. He's a good-looking dude who wears sneakers with his chinos like a trademark, but who today seems as greasy and shaken as if he's lost a bet. He doesn't push the hair out of his face when he talks, so we mentally do it for him. It's hard to hear the words through the mess of his delivery. We steal glances at Leslie, sure she must be mortified for him. She looks triumphant.

The gist, he explains, is that our attachment ratings will now be ranked. Those who consistently reach levels of moderate or above will continue with the study; those who reach high levels will be granted an array of privileges heretofore unknown to us. That's what he says, *heretofore unknown,* which makes us chuckle until we realize what he's saying. Or rather, what he hasn't said.

And the losers? we ask.

There are no losers, he says. Those who do not achieve a score of moderate or above will be re-incarcerated.

That stops us.

We look at Harry, who is failing to stifle a grin.

What are the privileges? someone asks.

Leslie's mentor brightens. Release from curfew, he says. No locks. Fewer mentor interventions. In a word, more freedom. And, by the way, the first to reach profound attachment will become our next Spokesmama.

Leslie no longer looks triumphant.

It's baffling, and we are accordingly skeptical. The mentors don't look at us. More freedom? we're thinking. That can't be legal. And it can't be good science.

One of the older mentors pipes up: The temptation to self-delude will be high, he says. We have tests to correct for inflated ratings.

He's warning us not to cheat.

Meaning they're upping the ante. Calling our bluff – we're either in the game, or we're out.

Meaning we have to seriously grapple with the question of what it means to attach to the wire children.

The mentors relax, message delivered, their eyes all a-glitter. We clench and stiffen, turning over the words *profound* and *attachment* like the explosives they are. We understand that the mentors are a hundred steps ahead of us, and we struggle to bridge the distance while playing like we don't notice it's there.

Come on now, we want to say. Be straight with us. This isn't our first rodeo.

Before they leave, the mentors pass out a flyer on Attachment Parenting and deliver one more incentive. The seven o-clock Pro-Hour of TV will now include a show called Carmen TV.

Fuck, someone says, long and slow, under her breath. Now that's an incentive.

Leslie sighs, screwed again by her lot. A good day for her is not actively hating her wire children. As we disperse, she says, Will you at least tell me what happens on Carmen TV? We assure her we will.

#

The wire children go down easy that night, as they often do on incentive nights. The mentors give us a taste of the reward – the first episode of Carmen TV – and then make it increasingly difficult to obtain. Tonight we're all parked in front of the TV by a quarter to seven, even, for the first time, Leslie. The courtyard glows blue. Those of us not on our scheduled cleanse pop bags of Faux Corn sprinkled with nutritional yeast, add lemon to our water bottles, and settle into our rockers. The show begins with an intro montage of Carmen's time here, cameos of ourselves we cheer over, a warning against reproducing the footage, a quick synopsis of the study – nothing we haven't been told – and then there she is, Carmen, looking both exactly and nothing like the woman we knew. Two things are clear right away: Carmen is not adjusting well to life on the outside, and Carmen has no idea she is being filmed.

There's no bag of Doritos. No reunion with her kids. No one greets her when the taxi drops Carmen off at a decrepit trailer. This is the place where it all went down. She stands outside a few minutes, and we cover our mouths. For god's sake, there's still police tape across the door. *Turn around,* we think. *Go anywhere else.* She looks behind her, but the taxi is gone. She gets out her key. Tears through the police tape. Opens the door.

It's the exact same trailer in the exact same condition she left it. This seems unlikely if not impossible, and yet it's true. The camera follows her face, but she appears not to register any memories or pain or even surprise associated with the scene. She doesn't recoil at what we imagine must be the overpowering stench of a squalid trailer left untouched for over a year. We're jolted into forbidden memories, flashbacks ripping through us. We've never once considered what happened to all the shit we left behind. The crib with its mess of cold blankets, the wrecked car in the driveway. Carseats still latched, spatter still constellating, rooms wreathed with the smell of smoke and diapers. We understand Carmen's reaction, which is not to pause over the mess, not to reflect or cry or call for help. She begins to clean. Fervently. That's the whole first episode. We watch with sick fascination. The degree of damage is hard to associate with the Carmen we know, the Carmen she was here, the role model of organization. All she has is a mostly-used, mostly congealed bottle of yellow dish soap. Her affect reveals nothing, though at one point she gags over a diaper balled into a football jersey in the closet. She throws out the diaper but puts the jersey into the oven. Produces a working lighter from somewhere and burns it.

Oven as purification tool: we understand this. The episode ends with Carmen dumping every dish and utensil into the front yard, squirting the pile with the last of the dish soap, and spraying it with a hose. She disappears behind the spray, and a legal message flashes across the screen that's gone before any of us can read it.

This is the end of the episode because there's no more soap. We don't know what she'll do next. We remember her answering her door in rubber gloves, how she made sugar scrubs for our birthdays. We clean our already-clean ovens out of respect for her that night.

The video does what we suppose it's intended to do. Shakes our confidence. Makes us realize that release is just "release," and that Carmen is still very much incarcerated. There is no real way to get out early.

Maybe we don't all literally have trailers full of shit. But we all have a shitload of forestalled atonement waiting for us outside this gate.

Wherever you are, we say. There you go.

Locked in our rooms, alone, we pace and hug our knees, chew fingernails and pull out eyelashes. We are sick for Carmen. We are scared for ourselves. What we wouldn't give for a drink or a pill or a vat of cheese dip. We picture the wire children and chant *love you love you love you* into our pillows. Sometimes we believe that we were chosen for this study because we are wired differently from other women. It's why we understand each other so well. Our brains go on- and offline all night, plaguing us with the same images in different dreams. Thorns in the turf. Mummified babies wrapped in fur. We walk along the water's edge as body parts wash up, and not a one of us can summon the energy to give a fuck, not even in dreams.

We wake sweaty, feeling the urge to nurse. But our breasts are limp, plundered. We are ravenous and uncomfortable, and it seems like Zee must be right about them putting things in our food. Hormones? Street drugs? We feel like we'll die if we don't get touched. We rush through breakfast, ignore the wire children, return to bed. For three days, we're soppy, drowsy hunks of meat. Our attachment scores hit record lows, and Carmen TV is all doomed job search and cold fast food breakfasts. Mallory sobs over Carmen. We all sob over Carmen, and none of us are the sobbing types.

Then it happens. On the fourth day, some unholy combination of deprivation and chemically-heightened desire pushes Patty over the edge. We're stunned to see her attachment score: high. Even a new episode of Carmen TV doesn't keep us from rushing to Patty's house, shocked and jealous and discouraged. Of all people, we say. She doesn't even like her wire child.

The Neighborhood

She answers the door looking downright matronly, the dose of success turning her usually-sallow face so rosy we'd swear she got ahold of makeup. We shunned Patty when she first got here, for her protection we thought, but she kept worming her way into our consciousness until we conceded that, even if she wasn't guilty, she wasn't innocent either. She was a mom; she was judged; that she'd been accused of the one thing she didn't do seemed incidental, in the end.

The rest of us were almost fortunate to have the convenience of a proper conviction.

We'd have all have found our way here somehow.

We crowd into Patty's playroom, Carmen TV muted in the background. Poor Carmen can't outshine Patty, especially now that we understand what a chump Carmen really is.

Patty goes through it step by step: I was kneading dough with my eyes closed, she says, blushing deeply. Maybe not kneading, to be honest. I was kind of stroking it. Here.

She reaches for a plastic bowl on top of the mini-fridge, removes the dishtowel cover. The dough has over-risen and collapsed. Our cabins come equipped with kitchen utensils and a binder of suggested projects. Home-baked bread is filed under Beginner, along with no-nut cookies and soft-boiled eggs. We shop at the whimsically-named on-site grocery, The Feed Store, which carries staples and approved substitutions, like carob chips and bean snacks, but no alcohol or caffeine or white sugar, though true to our natures, we've invented hooch versions of each.

Patty sets down the bowl and closes her eyes. She faces us, hand inside, and we start hooting and hollering all at once because we can see what she's up to. Patty, man, we yell. You're giving the dough a goddamn hand job!

Fucking Patty, we think. Who knew she had it in her?

She opens her eyes. Enjoying this. She says, So I'm all – you know – and my wire child sidles up to me, but I don't see her, right? She touches my thigh, and not in that stabby way, but gentle, like I taught her. She must've been practicing. So I feel this surge of emotion, like raw shit, you know? Like somebody poured warm butter all over me. And I know it's going to go away as soon as I think about it, so quick as I can, I say, 'I love you.' And it was true. Right in that moment, it was true.

Naw, we say. That was between you and the dough.

It was a transfer, she says. Account to account.

We get it. We're impressed. Patty has performed a sleight of hand, shifting the afterglow of her fantasy to the wire child so quickly that the emotion seemed simultaneous. We wonder if the mentors will question it, but they don't. We see that this system can be gamed after all.

Progress, we suppose, but the kind of thing you can pull off only a few times before the hidden cameras tip your hand.

Bottom line, Patty stumbled onto some luck. We figure she deserves it.

She rips out a piece of the magic dough for each of us to take home, and we spend the next days brainstorming, talking on the intercom, jotting in our Mama journals, re-reading the flyer on Attachment Parenting. We veto Kangaroo Care on account of how heavy the wire children are, as well as the serrated edges some of them develop on the playground. Sustained Eye Contact is a possibility, since the wire children are constructed to suggest facial features. They don't exactly have eyes, but we can tell where the eyes would be. Gazing into someone's eyes is a tried-and-true method of bonding, but it's hard to believe that gazing into where-eyes-would-be would have the same effect.

Zee says, I think it'd be easier if they did something for us.

I'm gonna teach mine to roll joints, Leslie says. Put these mofos to work.

Leslie is not going to win.

Then Mallory, who's never offered a solution, who up to this point didn't seem to have an original idea in her head, says, What if the children aren't the problem?

Mallory is the only one of us who had an Amber Alert on her. She was fierce about playground rules and made the same tired jokes about socks losing their mates that everyone did, but otherwise seemed pretty vapid.

We're like, Of course the children aren't the problem, the problem is that humans aren't programmed to bond with mechanical things, and she says, So what if they programmed us?

We're not following yet, but we shut the hell up and listen.

Didn't you ever used to feel like your phone controlled you? Maybe we could personalize the wire children. Like if you love someone, if you miss someone, you could teach your wire child to invoke that person, how a real child reminds you of something. Teach them to surprise you that way.

Sounds good, we say, but how. And that's when Mallory says, Wire School.

And we're like, right. *Wire School.*

The wire children know the basic I-love-yous and You're-the-best-moms, but they know nothing of the nuances of human emotion. So we teach them to surprise us, the way Patty's child surprised her.

This is an idea, we think, that has legs.

It's complicated and takes us a while to wrap our brains around it, but eventually we understand Mallory's real motive. It's not that she's smart. It's that she misses Carmen that much.

Mallory says: Write down the thing you wish someone would say. Write down three things. Give them to me by tomorrow. You'll see.

We file silently into the courtyard and back to our cabins. We watch the wire children play with trucks and dolls, study their jerky movements, listen to their babble. We imagine them hurt or dead and still don't care. It seems impossible to bypass the fact of their wires. We consider how they say they love us. How startled Carmen was that her wire child had cried.

Blissa, we remind ourselves.

Come here, we say, patting the plastic couch. How was your day? Do you know any jokes? What makes you shiver?

We feel more like mentors than mothers. We try to flush, to stammer, to increase our heartbeats. To conjure the heat we saw in Patty. We think about what we wish someone would say to us. Our own children, if they could talk. If we could talk to them.

We wonder if this might just work.

You're a good kid, we say, which is true. The wire children lack malice and recalcitrance. They are so genuine we'd like to smack them, if it wouldn't injure us to do so.

The wire children quiet at the unexpected attention. They sense a trap. When they finally speak, their words let us know they've put two and two together.

Where did Blissa's mom go?

She went back, we say. Does that scare you?

The wire children nod, though they know little of *back*. Their idiotic bravery is helpful; we feel a surge of protectiveness that could be the prelude to love. The wire children lead us closer to the edge of a precipice. We submerge thoughts that this is what they've been programmed to do; we don't even know if they can really be programmed; we experiment with belief.

I love you, the wire children say. We tolerate flashbacks of delivery rooms, bedrooms, interrogation rooms, courtrooms. The locked doors of our own childhoods. The clothes we loved like siblings, the siblings constant as furniture. Here's us, too old to still be in diapers, getting whipped for wetting the bed. Or rocking rag dolls to sleep. Or refusing to wear that jumper. Us at fifteen, buying pregnancy tests at the Dollar Store after church, or choking in the final stretch, or crawling out the window to meet the dickhead who'd pin us in the backseat. Us at twenty-five, promising to go cold turkey, or to try different meds, or to go out more, or to stay home. Holding our first babies, smiling for whatever camera was leveled at us, every newborn in every hospital dressed in the same pink and blue cap.

We scrub away our stretch marks and fill our memories with wire children.

A thought seeps in: maybe we'd have been better mothers if only we hadn't had real kids.

We tell the wire children that we are learning to love and getting closer every day, but of course, the wire children whimper. It's not what they want to hear.

We tell them, repeat after us: *this must be hard for you.*
I'm as much a victim as you are.
I just want us all to be happy.

We put into their "mouths" things our real children said, or things we'd wished they said, or things they might say if they could. *I forgive you.* And, *I'll never forgive you.* And, *We'll be okay.*

Repeat: *You're struggling, not bad.*
Repeat: *I know you didn't mean it.*

Hearing the words in the wire children's tinny voices burns us up inside. Our hearts harden into wire, which brings us closer to the wire children, sharing this organ with them. Wire hearts sprout wire veins. Wire veins grow over flesh ones, a slow but irreversible process. Our blood flows more efficiently. We move stiffly but with increased energy. Walking antennae, picking up waves and signals. The electrical currents of life quicken. We age without growing.

It seems almost real.

The wire children are disturbed by what we ask of them, but they do not resist. They go to bed uneasy, and finally, we think, we have made something. Call it corruption, call it original sin, call it consciousness – we've given them a piece of our world.

Leslie's scores stay low that night, but the rest of us are confidently moderate. Carmen TV is a non-starter. She doesn't come home. One full hour of her empty trailer.

#

Sarah tried to contact Carmen via the unlocked Wifi network but the message was returned as undeliverable. She only has access a few minutes at a time because she doesn't want anyone getting suspicious. She says we're famous. Convicts Or Martyrs? was one headline. The Father of New Motherhood, was another one. And another, Hard Time Harry. Half the population wants us burned at the stake, it turns out, and the other half wants to set us free.

Leslie's voice on the intercom that night is hoarse. She's been last on the attachment rankings all week. That's going to be me out there with Carmen, she says. They're going to feed me to the wolves.

Leslie, Leslie, we say. Have faith.

Don't fuck with me, she says. I'm a dead woman.

Stay positive, we say.

They don't understand, she says. I was never cut out to be a mom. I have nerve problems.

Don't, we say. Leslie.

My own mother, she starts, but we stop her. We all have mothers.

She's quiet. Our rooms are dark, locked until morning. The wire children are vulnerable and trusting in their perilous bodies. We would've never raised children as sheltered and stupid as they are.

The intercom crackles, and the power goes in and out. We hear engines and male voices long into the night. Sleep carries us fitfully to morning, and when the doors unlock, we're greeted by cameramen who motion us outside.

The Neighborhood

The wire children leave without our permission, not knowing to be wary of strange men.

We follow, not knowing to be wary of what's outside.

#

They've been instructed not to touch, but it takes Leslie all of fifteen seconds to lead one away from the herd. We don't blame her; we all feel lightheaded. It's not even because they're men, though they all are, but because they smell like fast food and convenience stores and cigarettes and coffee. And because, while we've stopped considering each other separate people, and while the mentors have always been a different species, these men are utterly, unforgivably human.

They're here to get footage for the commercial, they say, so we are to go about our usual business, not to perform or address the cameras, to try as much as we're able to forget they're there. Of course we can't, so after a half hour of instructing us to stop preening and posing in the courtyard, they switch to one-on-one interviews. Those don't work either, since we've been rehearsing canned responses in hope of becoming the next Spokesmama and all give the same answers. So then one of the cameramen – the unofficial leader, we can tell – goes rogue.

Hey, he shouts.

We stop posing and look at him.

Y'all have done some bad shit, right? Some real fucked up shit, and to your own kids. Hell, the whole world knows about it. Now you're living out in the woods with some crackpot evil scientist, or whatever he is, and I tell you what, people want to know what the hell is going on.

Jeff, one of the other cameramen says, You can't say that.

And Jeff says, Aw, fuck the script, man, the script ain't working.

Zee says, We're doing our time, and Jeff whips around and says, Are you?

You, he points at Leslie, Deep Throat. You locked your kids in a car, didn't you? You think Camp Rehab is a just punishment for that?

Leslie says nothing.

Ours were all high profile cases. There is nothing subtle about a dead kid in a car, or a malnourished toddler, or a shaken baby. The paths that led us to those moments, the accessories to our crimes, don't figure in, not to anyone who matters. The women we could've been are irrelevant. If we let ourselves track to the end of this thought, what we find is emptiness. If we try to trace back to the first wrong step, we arrive nowhere. We have our pick of causes: the inauspicious sign we were born under; the trauma transmitted through our genes; the dark closets of our childhoods; the wells of illness. Bad luck, bad choices. There was no one to protest back then. We understand that there is sustenance for these men in the solidity of the line that divides us. We huddle together, surrounding Leslie, our minds as one.

The wire children know nothing of protestors. They've never seen conflict like this before, and they aren't aware of our histories. We don't think they know they're an experiment, or that this isn't the whole world. They're characteristically quiet until one of Leslie's twins stands from his spot on the turf. If ever a stage was set for a revolt, it's this one. Jeff, the cameraman protestor, is less dangerous to us than the education he has just handed to the wire children.

We sizzle together, our wire hearts waiting on penance.

They had real kids? Leslie's wire child says to Jeff, and Jeff says, Dude, half these psychos killed their kids.

Leslie's wire child faces us. I understand now, he says.

Leslie says softly, unconvincingly, Sit down, Guardy.

Guardy says, It's not our fault. My god, this is huge. You're the broken ones, not us.

We close our eyes, wire vessels snapping free.

But you do try, Guardy continues. We see you trying.

It's a line Leslie taught him. We know that, and yet we're taken aback. We experience the rush of collective success. We all, every one of us, love Guardy in this moment.

Guardy moves toward the cameramen, and the head one, Jeff, takes a step back.

You're unkind, Guardy says. Get out of here. Leave our mothers alone.

They're not your mothers, Jeff says. And we have a job to do.

We get the feeling that what Jeff came to do is not what he was hired to do.

The other cameramen wait to see where this is going. We watch, fascinated and smitten and suddenly backgrounded.

You don't know the first thing about them, Jeff says.

Here's something you may not know about us, Guardy says. We're sharp.

He pokes Jeff. The other wire children fall in around him, their "fingers" and "knees" flashing.

We learn that the wire children are not dangerous except on accident and when threatened.

This is how we know we're still unfit for society: we wish for more gore. We want to see Jeff disemboweled, if only for the symbolism. We want the irony of our children killing for us. Guardy makes the threats, the younger ones go in for physical contact. Two girls, Zee's and Patty's kids, catch Jeff on the forearm, and the sight of blood makes the rest of the cameramen run for the back gate. They don't know the wire children can't really run, and they don't bother to look back.

They leave the gate open behind them, a detail only lost on us for the split second it takes the pendulum to swing from criminals to mothers and back.

We love you, we tell the wire children. It doesn't matter how, or how much, or how long. We'd kiss you if we could.

You belong out there, they say.

Beyond the gate is a forest of fir and cedar trees grown dense. The mentors will arrive soon enough, drive out in their vans, lock the locks.

This is our chance, we tell the children. Please understand.

We're all victims here, the wire children say. You deserve to be happy.

They return to the cabins. We look at the forest. We rehearse the whole montage: racing through the trees, panting, tripping over a root, the dogs after us. A miraculously unpoliced strip of Canadian border appearing like heaven, rays of sun across a field, maybe a rainbow. Then free and clear. Maybe years down the road, reconnecting with our kids. We imagine the call. *This is your mother.* No, *It's me, Mom.* Or maybe, *You don't remember me.* Or maybe, *You might have heard about me.*

Even in our fantasies, it's the wire children who respond.

Wherever you are, we say. There you go.

We are going to do it. We really are. It doesn't matter if it's a mistake. It doesn't matter if we end up worse off. We have to prove we're still human enough to try.

The gate stays open all day. The mentors never come.

#

Finally we shut the gate ourselves and fix dinner. Put the kids to bed. Our attachment scores are off the charts. Afterwards, we settle in for the next episode of Carmen TV.

She's back. She's trashed. There's some kind of house party in progress. Carmen is sprawled half-on, half-off the couch in her underwear. She's talking to a guy who is rubbing her ass and laughing at her.

It's hard to hear their voices, but we know what they're saying from the subtitles that run helpfully across the bottom of the screen.

Not a good idea, baby, he says.

You don't get it, she says. I *owned* it. I ruled that place.

Yeah, he says. I bet you did.

You don't get it, she says again. We couldn't give them human names.

Don't mean you're fixed, he says.

Don't mean I'm not, she says.

He turns her over and begins his work, and we shut off the TVs. We're in bed by ten.

ACKNOWLEDGEMENTS

Thanks to the editors of the journals in which these stories first appeared: "The Merm Prob" in *Gulf Coast*, "The Pedestal" in *The Tampa Review*, "You Don't Live Here" (as "Good Neighbor") in *Crazyhorse*, "The Stepmothers" in *Jeopardy*, "Dear Fairy Godmother" in *Barrelhouse*, "You're Not Going to Die" in *Kenyon Review*, "The Moral" (as "The Blush Reflex") in *Gulf Stream*, "Nobody Understands You Like Us" in *Nimrod International Journal of Poetry and Prose*, and "The Neighborhood" in *Granta*.

Thanks so much to Nick Courtright and Kyle McCord of Gold Wake Press for their incredibly hard work editing and publishing this book. Thanks also to Caitlin Clarkson for the use of her beautiful image for the cover.

Thanks to my colleagues and students at Western Washington University, and to the staff of Jeopardy Magazine, especially Hannah Newman.

And finally, thanks to Carol Guess for her friendship, inspiration, and advice; to Kami Westhoff for reading so many drafts of things and listening to even more ideas, and for being an all-around wonderful friend; to my family, for their constant love and support -- Joy and Andrew Langone, Tim Magee, Cassie and Jason Quest, Erin Magee, and Ben, Zoey, and Maggie Amick; and, especially, to Gus and Audrey

Magee-Kenney, who rekindled my affection for fairy tales, and who teach me all the time about love.

ABOUT GOLD WAKE PRESS

Gold Wake Press, an independent publisher, is curated by Nick Courtright and Kyle McCord. All Gold Wake titles are available at amazon.com, barnesandnoble.com, and via order from your local bookstore. Learn more at goldwake.com.

Available Titles:

Kyle Flak's *I Am Sorry for Everything in the Whole Entire Universe*
Keith Montesano's *Housefire Elegies*
David Wojciechowski's *Dreams I Never Told You & Letters I Never Sent*
Mary Quade's *Local Extinctions*
Adam Crittenden's *Blood Eagle*
Lesley Jenike's *Holy Island*
Mary Buchinger Bodwell's *Aerialist*
Becca J. R. Lachman's *Other Acreage*
Joshua Butts' *New to the Lost Coast*
Tasha Cotter's *Some Churches*
Nick Courtright's *Let There Be Light*
Kyle McCord's *You Are Indeed an Elk, But This is Not the Forest You Were Born to Graze*
Hannah Stephenson's *In the Kettle, the Shriek*
Kathleen Rooney's *Robinson Alone*
Erin Elizabeth Smith's *The Naming of Strays*

ABOUT THE AUTHOR

Kelly Magee is the author of *Body Language*, winner of the Katherine Anne Porter Prize for short fiction, as well as *With Animal*, co-written with Carol Guess, and *Your Sick*, co-written with Carol Guess and Elizabeth Colen. She teaches in the undergraduate and MFA programs in creative writing at Western Washington University. Follow her at kellyelizabethmagee.com.

CPSIA information can be obtained
at www.ICGtesting.com
Printed in the USA
FFOW03n1857180617
36754FF